A DARING FAITH
IN A HAZARDOUS WORLD

A Daring Faith In a Hazardous World:
Build A Courageous Lifestyle with Lee Roberson

Compiled by Lindsay Terry

Published by Ambassador Emerald International

A Daring Faith In A Hazardous World:
Build A Courageous Lifestyle with Lee Roberson

Numerous quotes are taken from Dr. Lee Roberson's books published by the Sword of the Lord Publishers, Murfreesboro, Tennessee. All of those books, and their dates, appear in a list presented in the back of this volume. The quotes are used by special permission.

The photographs were used with the permission of the
Lee Roberson Foundation
Chattanooga, Tennessee

All Scripture is quoted from the Authorized King James Version

Design and Composition by A & E Media - David Siglin

ISBN 1932307613

Published by the Ambassador Group

Ambassador Emerald International
427 Wade Hampton Blvd.
Greenville, SC 29609
USA
www.emeraldhouse.com

and

Ambassador Publications
Providence House
Ardenlee Street
Belfast BT6 8QJ
Northern Ireland
www.ambassador-productions.com

The colophon is a trademark of Ambassador

DEDICATION

To the memory of
Caroline Allen Roberson
the wife and constant companion of Dr. Lee
Roberson for 68 years. She went to heaven
June 26, 2005. She was 89 years of age.

ACKNOWLEDGMENTS

I would express my appreciation to my wife, Marilyn, who has been a constant encourager in this project, and more than that, a vital part of it. She, after both of us had agonized over the title for weeks, found the answer in one of Dr. Roberson's book, "The Faith That Moves Mountains." In it he wrote very persuasively about "A Daring Faith." She reminded me that Dr. Roberson's faith was just that. He also wrote of the hazards in this world that affect all of us. Marilyn also assisted in the categorizing of the quotations.

Three of Dr. Roberson's children, LeeAnne Nichols, John Roberson, and June Ormesher have been most cooperative and supportive. Buddy Nichols, LeeAnne's husband, has given valuable support, counsel and encouragement. June supplied some interesting pictures.

Samuel Lowry, Founder and CEO of Ambassador-Emerald International, was very encouraging, to the point of making a visit to our home in St. Augustine, Florida, during one of his trips to the States, to talk about the proposed book. He made many wonderful suggestions concerning the cover and the total make-up of the book. Including the photos was Sam's idea.

Brent Cook and Tim Lowry, in the Greenville offices of Ambassador-Emerald (home offices are in Belfast, Northern Ireland), have been most cooperative and helpful in putting the project together.

Mrs. Gloria Shadowens, Dr. Roberson's secretary for many years, kept me in communication with our hero. She also made a valuable contribution in supplying a number of the photos.

Lee Roberson, grandson of Dr. Roberson, also supplied a large number of photos from which to choose. Lee's computer abilities added greatly to the overall tone and quality of the book.

Dr. Bill Compton, my friend since childhood, was helpful and encouraging throughout the total process, supplying copies of some of Dr. Roberson's books and back issues of periodicals in which his writings appeared.

I am grateful to more than 30 Christian leaders who gave sincere endorsements of this volume and furnished wonderful statements of appreciation of Dr. Roberson's life and ministry. Their kind remarks appear throughout this anthology of the wit and wisdom of Dr. Roberson.

I want to express my appreciation to Dr. Shelton Smith and the Sword of the Lord Publishers for permission to reprint many of the quotations taken from books published by the Sword down through the years.

- Lindsay Terry

CONTENTS

INTRODUCTION

PREFACE

PROFILE OF LEE ROBERSON

THE QUOTATIONS OF LEE ROBERSON

BOOKS BY LEE ROBERSON

AFTERWORD

INTRODUCTION

It is with praise to God and gratitude in my heart that I say I have had the unique privilege of working closely with Dr. Lee Roberson for more than fifty years in the ministry of Tennessee Temple University and, since 1949, at the Highland Park Baptist Church of Chattanooga, Tennessee.

Never in all of those years did I see him flinch in the face of opposition; never did I see him show the slightest sign of compromise when called upon to sacrifice a conviction; and, never did I see him waver in his faith when the "oil in the cruse" and the "meal in the barrel" were running low.

Dr. Roberson has a great love for God and His Christ, and an unquenchable thirst for the Bible. His desire to make God's Word known swept from his messages through the pews of the church, into "the byways and hedges" of the community, and unto the "uttermost parts of the earth."

Dr. Roberson's love for lost souls manifested itself in every message he preached, whether it was from his pulpit, at a funeral service, a wedding, a college chapel service, or a Sunday School picnic. The tenderness of this man's heart was not always visible to the public. It went beyond what one saw in his work for Camp Joy, which he founded in 1946, and where over 100,000 children have attended free of charge, and were all given the Gospel of Christ.

World Wide Faith Missions, with hundreds of missionaries supported; Union Gospel Mission for the homeless in downtown Chattanooga; 70 branch churches; WDYN, a 100,000 watt radio station; The Evangelist, a widely read periodical; Tennessee Temple University and Temple Baptist Theological Seminary, with graduates serving around the world; a high school; an elementary school; the authoring of approximately 46 books; and millions of miles traveled to preach in churches near and far, are all varying aspects of Dr. Roberson's vast ministry.

One can never really come close to knowing the heart of this man of God until kneeling with him at the side of a penitent sinner, or seeing him when he opened his purse to aid a person in need, or observing him as he wept with a homesick student, away from his family for the first time. Even in his time of retirement from pastoral responsibilities, he was writing cards to the bereaved, visiting them and the elderly in their homes, and making his way to the hospitals to pray with the sick.

Never has any person been so blessed of God as have I in being allowed to serve at the side of a man of God such as Dr. Lee Roberson. I praise the dear Lord for every blessing that has come to me and my family through our association.

- J. R. Faulkner
November 19, 2005

PREFACE

It has been my privilege to know Dr. Lee Roberson for more than fifty years.

When I was sixteen years of age my pastor, Covell Keenum, took me to a Bible Conference in Toccoa Falls, Georgia. I saw Lee Roberson for the first time. I will never forget the commanding voice which filled the auditorium, the stateliness of the man, and his sincere preaching.

Two years later, I actually met him when I became a freshman at Tennessee Temple University. As a student I was able to observe him for six years -- through college and seminary. During my latter seminary years, I had the joy of traveling with him to special meetings as a singer and trumpet player. He was always available to counsel with me, no matter what my need or problem might have been.

My wife, Marilyn, also a Temple grad, and I were married in the living room of his home on July 1, 1955. It was a short "Dr. Roberson ceremony," but very meaningful to us. Through all of these years, he and Mrs. Roberson have been our dear friends. It has been our privilege to sing during a number of his meetings since our college and seminary days. I have also had the opportunity to return to Highland Park Baptist Church and to TTU to sing or lecture on sixteen occasions.

Since my student days, I have been totally convinced of Dr. Roberson's commitment to the Lord's service. He is also a man of extreme discipline in his personal life and his ministry schedule. His work ethic is exemplary. During a chapel service I once observed him holding to the podium to steady himself after traveling all night to get back to speak to the students. I have seen him speak when he had not undressed for more than two days. Student chapel was a major priority.

Like Theodore Roosevelt and Barry Goldwater before him, Dr. Roberson learned early on that he only required about four hours of sleep each night. I asked him about that on one occasion, in earlier years, and he said, "I go to bed at midnight and read until 1:30 or 2:00 a.m." Four hours later he was up getting ready for breakfast which was at 6:30 a.m. He did, however, according to his daughters, LeeAnne Nichols and June Ormesher, take a nap after lunch before engaging in other activities. June said, "Early in his ministry a doctor had told him that he could add 10 to 20 years to his life by resting for an hour in the middle of the day." Mrs. Roberson, who passed away in 2005, told Marilyn in a conversation several years ago, "We keep the same schedule the year round, even on vacation."

As for exercise, June related, "When driving to the hospitals dad would park some distance away and walk. At the hospital he rode elevators up and walked down." He took time to visit the church members in the local hospitals each afternoon when he was not traveling. Even with the care of the Church and the schools and a myriad of other responsibilities, when his schedule would permit, he would attend student activities such as recitals and ball games. The whole of it was very meaningful to him.

Dr. Roberson has been a leader of men, "walking the point," for more than three quarters of a century. After his college and seminary days, he continued his study of theology and became an avid reader. The books he has devoured would equal a sizable library in number. June said, "The great evangelist, Hyman Appelman, often sent him large boxes of books. My Dad made a point of reading each one and then giving them to the TTU library." The knowledge gained through building, the study of the Bible, reading, preaching, pastoring, practical experience, personal sorrow, sickness, and the observing of humanity around him equipped him to be a most effective leader.

- Lindsay Terry
March 24, 2006

A PROFILE OF LEE ROBERSON'S LIFE

Lee Roberson was born to Charles and Dora Roberson on November 24, 1909, in a two room cabin on a small farm near English, Indiana. Two years later his family moved to a farm near Louisville, Kentucky. At age fourteen he was led to Christ by his Sunday school teacher, Mrs. Daisy Hawes. He joined the Cedar Creek Baptist Church near Louisville, and was baptized by Pastor J. N. Binford. The church was small but aggressive, active and Bible-centered. He carefully observed the faithfulness, zeal, and compassion of Pastor Binford. Those lessons helped him form a mindset for future years. He was called to preach at eighteen years of age.

Young Lee Roberson entered Old Bethel College in Russellville, Kentucky, in 1928, working his way through by washing dishes and cleaning floors. A year later he transferred to the University of Louisville, where he graduated with a major in history. He then entered Southern Baptist Theological Seminary in Louisville and studied under the renowned Dr. A. T. Robertson. He was a conscientious student of the Bible and on one occasion, read the entire Greek New Testament.

He also studied at Cincinnati Conservatory of Music with the famed vocal instructor John Samples and was in demand as a singer. He was a staff soloist for Radio Stations WHAS in Louisville and WSM in Nashville, Tennessee. He turned down offers that would have led to a financially profitable future in secular music. He was sure in his heart that God had called him into the ministry.

At this point I will let Dr. Roberson relate the remaining sequence of events in his life, as recorded in his book, *A Winner Never Quits and a Quitter Never Wins*, published by the Sword of the Lord Publishers in 1994.

"My first full-time work was at the Virginia Avenue Baptist Church of Louisville, Kentucky. My pastor was L. W. Benedict from New York State, a graduate of the Southern

Baptist Seminary. There is where I got my first lesson on the importance of visitation. Brother Benedict kept me visiting night and day, covering the west end of Louisville."

"In addition to visitation, I directed the church music. I worked at the church's radio station, WLAP (We Love All People). I taught a Sunday school class (all of this before I was twenty). At the same time, I attended school at the University of Louisville and took some classes at the Southern Baptist Seminary. (My salary was $40.00 per month. This was in the Depression days.)"

"My first pastorate was at the Germantown Baptist Church, located at the edge of Memphis, Tennessee. Virginia Avenue Baptist Church ordained me. The ordination sermon in 1932 was by my first pastor, Rev. J. N. Binford."

"Thirty-two people were present on my first Sunday morning at Germantown. The church was organized about 1865. The building was old but beautiful. I remained at my first church one year. There I baptized many converts. There we built a Sunday school building and filled it with happy people. We grew."

"And then, a big mistake! I stepped out of the will of God. Without prayer and meditation, I accepted the position of assistant pastor of the Temple Baptist Church in Memphis. I experienced three months of misery. Soon after taking the position, I knew I was out of God's will. The pastor insisted that I stay, but I had to leave. Then followed five months of emptiness -- no church, no work."

"I was invited to speak at the Greenbrier Baptist Church in Greenbrier, Tennessee, twenty-two miles from Nashville. The little church called me. This time I waited on God. I prayed earnestly. The Lord directed me to take the church. I spent three happy years there as pastor. I lived in a tiny room at the back of the church. There was no bathroom, no telephone -- just one room; but I was happy, for I was in His will."

"In 1935, I was called to be the Evangelist for the Birmingham (Alabama) Baptist Association. I was elected by the association. I received no salary but love offerings from my meetings. I preached fifty-five revivals in churches and tents and enjoyed a great season of soulwinning for two years."

"In 1937, I was called to pastor the First Baptist Church of Fairfield, Alabama, adjoining Birmingham. That year I got married! (He and Caroline Allen were wed on October 9, 1937.) I entered the work of the pastorate again. For five years we worked with the Fairfield church. It grew from 125 to an average of 850. Evangelism, both public and private, was pushed. The Sunday school was expanded. There was growth in every division of the work. We were very happy."

"But one Sunday a pulpit committee appeared from Chattanooga. The Highland Park Baptist Church there had endeavored to get Dr. John C. Cowell of the Central Baptist Church of Decatur, Alabama, to be their pastor; but when he refused their offer, he gave the committee my name." (My dad, Marvin J. Terry, was led to the Lord by Dr. Cowell in Decatur.)

"The committee heard me preach and invited me to Highland Park for a service. I did visit the church for one Sunday morning in October of 1942. The church called me, but I was not sure of God's will. I waited. I prayed. Dr. T. W. Callaway of Chattanooga came to see me to add his emphasis to the call."

"It was a struggle, but I finally knew the will of God and accepted the call. I knew it was God's will. I never doubted this."

This ministry continued for forty years and six months. The church grew to a membership of more than 25,000, with 61,000 converts baptized. It became one of the largest and most influential churches in America with a total attendance of 10,000 or more on some occasions. During the years Dr. Roberson was at HPBC, he also preached almost every week to one or two other churches somewhere in the United States. He also led in the starting of 50 branch churches or chapels in the greater Chattanooga area.

In 1946, Dr. Roberson founded Tennessee Temple Schools, a junior college and a Bible school. In 1948 the college expanded to four years, later becoming Tennessee Temple University. Temple Baptist Theological Seminary was also founded in 1948. From these institutions, thousands of young people have been and continue to be sent out as pastors, evangelists, and missionaries. Many more are music ministers, teachers, and business professionals.

HPBC launched World-Wide Faith Missions which has supported missionaries around the world. HPBC now operates Faith Missions Agency, enabling and assisting local churches in fulfilling the Great Commission. Hundreds of missionaries are still supported.

In addition to the University, Bible School and Seminary, a grade school and a high school were also started in Chattanooga.

Following the death of his baby daughter, Joy, in 1946, he founded Camp Joy, a Bible camp near Chattanooga, "where boys and girls begin to live." Over 3,000 children enjoy a week at the camp each summer. At the time of this writing, Camp Joy continues to have a great ministry and has, over the years, hosted almost 100,000 children and teenagers.

In 1950, Pastor Roberson led the launching of Union Gospel Mission in downtown Chattanooga, with the capability of sleeping many homeless people and which continues to operate to this day. Thousands of needy families have been fed and continue to receive food and clothing. A weekly radio broadcast from the Mission can be heard each Sunday morning.

In 1956, Dr. Roberson was instrumental in helping to start Southwide Baptist Fellowship, a "family" of churches and pastors which meet in an annual conference. More than 1,000 churches have appeared in their directory.

For many years he also maintained a daily radio ministry, "Gospel Dynamite," and a Sunday night broadcast, "The Back Home Hour." In 1968, Radio Station WDYN-FM went on the air in the tri-state area. With a great increase in power, it continues to send the Gospel of Christ to the west Tennessee, north Alabama, and northeast Georgia areas. Several television outlets have been added in the past several years, greatly increasing the media outreach of HPBC.

For all but the first two years of his total ministry at HPBC Dr. Roberson had Dr. J. R. Faulkner by his side as his Associate. J. R. Faulkner is one of the most talented men on the face of the earth. In addition to being a knowledgeable Sunday school builder, he is a masterful song leader, an accomplished artist, a promotions expert, poet, and a gifted preacher. Once when Dr. Roberson was asked, "What would you do if you lost J. R. Faulkner?" The reply was, "I'd hire six men and go right on." After Dr. Roberson's retirement, Dr. Faulkner became the pastor of HPBC for approximately two years.

Since Lee Roberson's retirement in 1983, he has given his time to writing and to preaching in churches and conferences in the United States as well as other countries. During much of that time he has averaged speaking in more than 125 churches each year, often several times in each location during two and three day meetings. In those sessions he seeks to encourage pastors and Christian leaders, giving them methods for increasing the important work of the Sunday school and of reaching more people through visitation, preaching, teaching, and personal soulwinning.

Dr. Roberson has authored approximately 45 books, and for many years he published *The Evangelist*, a weekly periodical with 73,000 readers. Dr. John R. Rice called him the "Spurgeon of our day." Billy Graham said of him in 1953, "Lee Roberson is doing more for God than any other man in America."

At the time of this writing, he is Pastor Emeritus of the Church and Chancellor of the University and has been preaching for 78 years. He continues to "walk the point" for thousands who love, respect, trust, and follow him.

THE QUOTATIONS OF
Lee Roberson

On the following pages we joyfully present an anthology of the wit and wisdom of Dr. Roberson. Use the truths capsuled in these quotations to help you develop a daring faith and a courageous lifestyle which will allow you to face life's challenges in a hazardous world.

The quotes are presented along with an appropriate, substantiating Scripture and the name and the year of the particular book, written by Dr. Roberson, from which it was taken. A complete listing of Dr. Roberson's books is presented in the back of this volume.

Lee Roberson is doing more for God than any other man in America.

- Billy Graham, Evangelist

This statement was made during Dr. Graham's visit to Chattanooga, Tennessee, in 1953. His primary reason for going to that city was to preach in the large city-wide crusade, but his visit also gave him the opportunity to see first-hand something of the world-wide ministry and accomplishments of Dr. Roberson and the Highland Park Baptist Church where he was pastor for more than forty years.

A

ALCOHOL

The devil has encouraged strong drink until millions are now alcoholics.
— *Fireworks Don't Last,* 1982

"Wine is a mocker, strong drink is raging: and whosoever is deceived thereby is not wise." Proverbs 20:1

ANXIETY

The life of faith excludes worry. Worry is sin.
— *Fireworks Don't Last,* 1982

"Be careful for nothing; but in every thing by prayer and supplication with thanksgiving let your requests be made known unto God. And the peace of God, which passeth all understanding, shall keep your hearts and minds through Christ Jesus." Philippians 4:6-7

APATHY

The commands of Christ are sharp and clear, but the response of His people is often measured and lifeless.
— *"The Hallelujah Chorus" In One Verse,* 1996

"He that saith, I know him, and keepeth not his commandments, is a liar, and the truth is not in him. But whoso keepeth his word, in him verily is the love of God perfected." 1 John 2:4-5

ATTITUDE

If we are going to come before God with a positive approach, then we must be right, and we cannot be made right unless we are willing to face our needs.
— *Coming to Chattanooga-Soon,* 1980

"Casting all your care upon him; for he careth for you." 1 Peter 5:7

ASSURANCE

Make sure that you are fully aware of all that you have in Jesus.
— A Winner Never Quits and A Quitter Never Wins, 1994

"For the which cause I also suffer these things: nevertheless I am not ashamed: for I know whom I have believed, and am persuaded that he is able to keep that which I have committed unto him against that day." 2 Timothy 1:12

A memento at a preaching anniversary.

Along with being an effective soul-winner, Dr. Lee Roberson is a faithful preacher of the Word, an inspiring leader, a godly example, a dependable friend, and a gifted recruiter of men and women for the Gospel ministry. During the forty years of our friendship, I have never been in his presence without feeling encouraged and enriched. I don't know how many times I have quoted his statement, "Everything rises and falls on leadership." His humility and faith exalt Jesus Christ. He has made a lasting impression on my life and ministry and I am grateful. This anthology of quotations from Dr. Roberson will be a permanent source of spiritual wisdom and guidance for generations to come.

- Warren W. Wiersbe, Author and Bible Teacher

B

BIBLE

Every portion of God's Word has a spiritual significance for all people of all ages.
— Fireworks Don't Last, 1982

"As newborn babes, desire the sincere milk of the word, that ye may grow thereby:" 1 Peter 2:2

It is amazing how much space is spent in the Word of God exhorting the weak.
— Mr. Saint and Mr. Sinner Look at the Second Coming of Christ, 1963

"Strengthen ye the weak hands, and confirm the feeble knees." Isaiah 35:3

It is the Word of God that gives the heart a passion for souls and brings conviction to the lost.
— Diamonds in the Rough, 1997

"For the word of God is quick, and powerful, and sharper than any two-edged sword, piercing even to the dividing asunder of soul and spirit, and of the joints and marrow, and is a discerner of the thoughts and intents of the heart." Hebrews 4:12

Reading the Bible is a healing balm for the soul.
— Touching Heaven, 1991

"O how love I thy law! it is my meditation all the day." Psalms 119:97

There must be a book, and that Book is the Bible. I have never met any situation yet for which it has not had the answer.
— Fireworks Don't Last, 1982

"Trust in the LORD with all thine heart; and lean not unto thine own understanding. In all thy ways acknowledge him, and he shall direct thy paths." Proverbs 3:5-6

The Bible must be burned into hearts. This is the only way. Hearts must be branded by the message of God's Word.
— Start the Fire, 1986
"Thy word have I hid in mine heart, that I might not sin against thee."
Psalms 119:11

If you read very far into the Word of God, you will find the Sword cutting into your very life and being. It will cut into the swollen and puffy places.
— The Evangelist, 1949
"For whatsoever things were written aforetime were written for our learning, that we through patience and comfort of the Scriptures might have hope."
Romans 15:4

The Bible is the book that comforts and challenges, gives light to our pathway, strengthens us in our hour of weakness, gives food for the soul and refreshment for the heart.
— Diamonds in the Rough, 1997
"And take the helmet of salvation, and the Sword of the Spirit, which is the Word of God." Ephesians 6:17

The Christian has two guides for his life, the Holy Spirit and the Word of God. The Word of God is our compass through the stormy seas.
— Are You Tired of Living?, 1945
"Thy word is a lamp unto my feet, and a light unto my path." Psalms 119:105

When you are weary and tired, sitting down with the Word is like sitting down to a satisfying meal, or drinking a glass of cool water when you are thirsty.
— Are You Tired of Living?, 1945
"My soul melteth for heaviness: strengthen thou me according unto thy word." Psalms 119:28

The Word of God will keep you from sin, it will keep your soul on fire, and it will give you a concern for others.
— Two Dogs and Peace of Mind, 1974
"But his word was in mine heart as a burning fire shut up in my bones, and I was weary with forbearing, and I could not stay." Jeremiah 20:9

Most of us have discovered that to open the Bible and hear God's voice is to be corrected of some weakness, some misdemeanor, or some sin.
— A Winner Never Quits and A Quitter Never Wins, 1994
"For whom the Lord loveth he chasteneth, and scourgeth every son whom he receiveth." Hebrews 12:6

Dr. Lee Roberson is among the handful of pastors most used by the Lord in the history of Chattanooga. The highest compliment was paid to him by a local business man who attended his church: "Lee Roberson never preaches to the giraffes. That is why I go there. That is why everyone can understand him. That is why there are so many conversions. And he always preaches for conversions.

- Ben Haden, former Pastor, First Presbyterian Church, Chattanooga, Tennessee. Speaker on "Changed Lives" TV-Radio for 33 years.

We must stand for the Word of God, stand for the work of God, stand without wavering, without flinching and without faltering.

— The Gold Mine, 1996

"Wherefore take unto you the whole armour of God, that ye may be able to withstand in the evil day, and having done all, to stand. Stand therefore, having your loins girt about with truth, and having on the breastplate of righteousness;" Ephesians 6:13

The Bible is the victory Book! Read the Word. Memorize the Word. Saturate your life in the Word. Let the Word be your guide.

— Two Dogs and Peace of Mind, 1974

"Be ye doers of the Word, and not hearers only..." James 1:22

Quite often we read the Word of God but fail to get the significance of what God is saying. We miss the beauty of His Word. We miss seeing it with our own eyes. We also miss our obligations to the One who created such beauty for us to enjoy.

— Diamonds in the Rough, 1997

"And let the beauty of the LORD our God be upon us: and establish thou the work of our hands upon us; yea, the work of our hands establish thou it." Psalms 90:17

The Word of God is a living seed, an incorruptible seed with life and power. Jeremiah compared the power of this seed of the Word to a hammer that "breaketh the rock in pieces."

— The Gold Mine, 1996

"Is not my word like as a fire? saith the LORD; and like a hammer that breaketh the rock in pieces?" Jeremiah 23:29

Put your life under God's x-ray. Let the word of God reach into your heart and search it out.
— Fireworks Don't Last, 1982

"The entrance of Thy words giveth light; it giveth understanding unto the simple." Psalm 119:130

People turn away from the Bible because it tells man that all of his righteousnesses are as filthy rags in God's sight.
— The Gold Mine, 1996

"But we are all as an unclean thing, and all our righteousnesses are as filthy rags; and we all do fade as a leaf; and our iniquities, like the wind, have taken us away." Isaiah 64:6

It is good to have a Bible answer for every question! This is the Word of God, inspired and infallible! Upon this Word we can pillow our head and find peace in our hearts.
— People: A Book About Bible People, 1983

"Blessed are they that keep his testimonies, and that seek him with the whole heart." Psalms 119:2

The Bible gives untouched pictures of even God's greatest men and women. This is but another proof of the divine inspiration of this Book. If man had written the Bible, many things would have been omitted. Virtues would have been extolled and vices covered up or forgotten.
— People: A Book About Bible People, 1983

"I will praise thee with uprightness of heart, when I shall have learned thy righteous judgments." Psalms 119:7

I am not interested in religious exercises! They annoy me, provoke me, and destroy within me that which should cry after the Lord. There may be a meaning to religious exercises (mere form of reading the Bible and praying or reciting creeds), but I don't know what it is.
— Touching Heaven, 1991

"Wherewithal shall a young man cleanse his way? by taking heed thereto according to thy word." Psalms 119:9

Presenting one of thousands of diplomas at TTU

Dr. Lee Roberson is a giant of faith and faithfulness whose words of exhortation and encouragement will stir your heart and bless your life. In the past 100 years only a handful of men have touched so many people so strongly and so often. Whatever he has to say should be heard and heeded by all of us.

- Shelton L. Smith, President and Editor, Sword of the Lord

C

CHARACTER

The very elevation of a man's character, no matter how social and humanitarian he may be and how noble his efforts for mankind, may repel men as well as attract them.
—— "The Hallelujah Chorus" In One Verse, 1996

"What fruit had ye then in those things whereof ye are now ashamed? for the end of those things is death. But now being made free from sin, and become servants to God, ye have your fruit unto holiness, and the end everlasting life." Romans 6:21-22

CHASTENING

Chastening, rightly borne, will make strong Christians.
—— Compassion Unlimited

"If ye endure chastening, God dealeth with you as with sons; for what son is he whom the father chasteneth not?" Hebrews 12:7

CHILDREN

I spend a lot of time with children. I love them. God loves them. I have one fear in my heart, and that is that I might not always be a good influence for them.
—— Are You Tired of Living?, 1945

"But whoso shall offend one of these little ones which believe in me, it were better for him that a millstone were hanged about his neck, and that he were drowned in the depth of the sea." Matthew 18:6

CHRIST

Christ was the same in every part of His ministry, and He is the same today. He has the same compassion and the same yearning soul. He changes not.
— "The Hallelujah Chorus" In One Verse, 1996
"Jesus Christ the same yesterday, and to day, and for ever." Hebrews 13:8

Without Christ, we have no key to the various mysteries of life. Without Him, we have no answers to the problems of life. In Christ, we have the master key to all mysteries, questions, and puzzles.
— The Key to Victorious Living, 1978
"I am the vine, ye are the branches: He that abideth in me, and I in him, the same bringeth forth much fruit: for without me ye can do nothing." John 15:5

Oh, my friends, we can never exhaust the subject of Christ! We can never come to the end of our discussion of His worthiness, His loveliness, and His power.
— Start the Fire, 1986
"And Jesus came and spake unto them, saying, All power is given unto me in heaven and in earth." Matthew 28:18

Christ did not come to clean up the foul smelling evils of the Roman government. He came as a Lamb to the slaughter, to die for the redemption of all who would believe on His name.
— Are You Tired of Living? 1945
"He was oppressed, and he was afflicted, yet he opened not his mouth: he is brought as a lamb to the slaughter, and as a sheep before her shearers is dumb, so he openeth not his mouth." Isaiah 53:7

Christ is the most magnificent figure of all times. His name is more imperial than Caesar's; more musical than Beethoven's; more elegant than Demosthenes; more conquering than Napoleon. The Satan who fought the Lord Jesus when He walked upon this earth has been fighting Christ and the work of Christ ever since. Yet it still remains that Christ is the most majestic figure of all times.

— The Key to a Changed Life, 1978

"Wherefore God also hath highly exalted him, and given him a name which is above every name:" Philippians 2:9

CHRIST-LIKENESS

The Christian life is the hidden life. The hidden life is the safe life, the justified life, the joyful life, the comfortable life, and the fruitful life.

— Preaching to America, 1999

"I am crucified with Christ: nevertheless I live; yet not I, but Christ liveth in me: and the life which I now live in the flesh I live by the faith of the Son of God, who loved me, and gave himself for me." Galatians 2:20

We become more like Christ as we suffer for Him. Note carefully, you are not to make yourself suffer, but suffering will come if you live a true, consecrated life.

— Fireworks Don't Last, 1982

"Yea, and all that will live godly in Christ Jesus shall suffer persecution." 2 Timothy 3:12

As a young preacher and pastor, I used to wait each week to get my copy of "The Evangelist" and was always inspired by the hand of God upon Dr. Lee Roberson and the Highland Park Baptist Church. His dedication continues to be an inspiration to me to this day. If ever a man is finishing strong it is Lee Roberson. He is synonymous with "leadership" and like King David he has led us all "with the integrity of his heart and the skillfulness of his hands."

- O. S. Hawkins, President, GuideStone Financial Resources of the SBC, Former pastor of First Baptist Church, Dallas, Texas

CHRISTIAN GROWTH

In life there are some things that are elective, and we can decide to take them or refuse them. Obedience is an elective course, so is the Lordship of Christ, discipline in life, and devotion to Christ.
— Preaching to America, 1999
"But speaking the truth in love, may grow up into him in all things, which is the head, even Christ:" Ephesians 4:15

Whether we like it or not, we are going to school every day. We may fail or we may succeed, but we are going to school. Furthermore, there is no cessation of this. It lasts as long as life itself.
— Preaching to America, 1999
"Study to shew thyself approved unto God, a workman that needeth not to be ashamed, rightly dividing the word of truth." 2 Timothy 2:15

A great Christian has faith, rock-ribbed convictions, vision, endurance, submission and compassion.
— "The Hallelujah Chorus" In One Verse, 1996

"But grow in grace, and in the knowledge of our Lord and Saviour Jesus Christ. To him be glory both now and for ever. Amen." 2 Peter 3:18 "And of some have compassion, making a difference:" Jude 1:22

CHRISTIAN WALK

This is the sadness of the day. We are teaching people how to walk, how to make money, how to have a good time, but we are not teaching them the Christian walk — the walk that comes only through knowing Jesus Christ, the blessed Saviour.
— The Gold Mine, 1996

"And make straight paths for your feet, lest that which is lame be turned out of the way; but let it rather be healed." Hebrews 12:13

CHURCH

My friend, you can't put your life into a greater work than to unite with a local church and give yourself in service to it. Every work that you do will pay dividends here and hereafter.
— Death and After, 1954

"Christ also loved the church, and gave himself for it;" Ephesians 5:25

The first step to a backslidden life is missing church.
— Death and After, 1954

"Not forsaking the assembling of ourselves together, as the manner of some is; but exhorting one another: and so much the more, as ye see the day approaching." Hebrews 10:25

I am afraid that too many churches have endeavored to make their architecture and programs compare with the airy grace of a country club. We have gone so far for comfort, for ease and for pleasure, that we have turned away from the straight course marked out for us by our Saviour.

— The Gold Mine, 1996

"Lead me, O LORD, in thy righteousness because of mine enemies; make thy way straight before my face." Psalms 5:8

COMMITMENT

Strong Christians will be mature, committed, and unselfish.

— "The Hallelujah Chorus" In One Verse, 1996

"But grow in grace, and in the knowledge of our Lord and Saviour Jesus Christ. To him be glory both now and for ever. Amen." 2 Peter 3:18

Some of the world's greatest people have been lonely men and women who committed themselves to the hand of God. They discovered that the higher they climbed, the lonelier they became.

— "The Hallelujah Chorus" In One Verse, 1996

"Ye have not chosen me, but I have chosen you, and ordained you, that ye should go and bring forth fruit, and that your fruit should remain: that whatsoever ye shall ask of the Father in my name, he may give it you." John 15:16

Paul, the apostle, was reckless for God.

— Start the Fire, 1986

"But none of these things move me, neither count I my life dear unto myself, so that I might finish my course with joy, and the ministry, which I have received of the Lord Jesus, to testify the gospel of the grace of God." Acts 20:24

COMPANIONS

You WILL become like those with whom you associate.
— Advice to students of Tennessee Temple University

"He that walketh with wise men shall be wise: but a companion of fools shall be destroyed." Proverbs 13:20

COMPASSION

We are untouched by the tragedy of the lostness of men.
— Diamonds In the Rough, 1997

"I looked on my right hand, and beheld, but there was no man that would know me: refuge failed me; no man cared for my soul." Psalms 142:4

COMPASSION OF CHRIST

Jesus Christ was generous toward the vilest of sinners, the worst of enemies, and the poorest of men.
— "The Hallelujah Chorus" In One Verse, 1996

"All we like sheep have gone astray; we have turned every one to his own way; and the LORD hath laid on him the iniquity of us all." Isaiah 53:6

I am grateful for this encouraging book of quotations by Dr. Roberson. The Lord has used him in a mighty way in all our lives. I deeply appreciate the honor given him and the contribution made to the work of the Lord by providing this resource.

- Clarence Sexton, President, Crown College, Pastor, Temple Baptist, Knoxville, Tennessee

COMPLACENCY

Overconfidence leads to a neglect of spiritual exercises. Foolish self-confidence will lead one to turn away from the Bible and prayer and make him imagine that he is spiritually strong without these things.
— "The Hallelujah Chorus" In One Verse, 1996
"Woe to them that are at ease in Zion, and trust in the mountain of Samaria, which are named chief of the nations, to whom the house of Israel came!" Amos 6:1

CONFIDENCE

We need certain confidence in ourselves and in our God, but there is a danger of overconfidence. It is overconfidence that leads us to think all is well when we may have some serious deficiencies in our lives.
— "The Hallelujah Chorus" In One Verse, 1996
"Wherefore let him that thinketh he standeth take heed lest he fall."
1 Corinthians 10:12

CONSECRATION

Let me give you seven words to live by: faith, obedience, service, compassion, faithfulness, conse-cration, and watchfulness.
— A Winner Never Quits and A Quitter Never Wins, 1994
"Blessed art thou, O LORD: teach me thy statutes." Psalms 119:12

If your life is aligned with the forces of righteousness, you will win here and hereafter.
— Are You Tired of Living?, 1945
"Far above all principality, and power, and might, and dominion, and every name that is named, not only in this world, but also in that which is to come:" Ephesians 1:21

I believe that consecration will come by remembering that one day we shall stand before the Lord Jesus Christ.
— Start the Fire, 1986
"So then every one of us shall give account of himself to God." Romans 14:12

CONTENTMENT

Yes, I think that it is evident from the Word of God that our Lord wants you to have contentment. He wants you to have peace in your heart. I believe this is a part of contentment.
— 7 Life Changing Statements, 1972
"Peace I leave with you, my peace I give unto you: not as the world giveth, give I unto you. Let not your heart be troubled, neither let it be afraid." John 14:27

CONVERSION

Quite often the skeptic is a man with a hungry heart.
— Death and After? 1954
"Blessed are they which do hunger and thirst after righteousness: for they shall be filled." Matthew 5:6

CONVICTIONS

The Christian must not sidestep any issue. With courage, face every question. Don't foolishly imagine you can live righteously without enemies.
—— Preaching to America, 1999
"Yea, and all that will live godly in Christ Jesus shall suffer persecution."
2 Timothy 3:12

There is nothing wrong in a Christian holding a place of influence in government or in any realm of society. Quite often such a place will give opportunities for service to God, but we know quite well that only a few can occupy such a position without compromising their convictions.
—— The King's Water Boy
"Wherefore seeing we also are compassed about with so great a cloud of witnesses, let us lay aside every weight, and the sin which doth so easily beset us, and let us run with patience the race that is set before us," Hebrews 12:1

A Christian cannot walk two ways at one time. He must either walk in the way of the cross or the way of the world.
—— The Big 90, 1999
"No man can serve two masters: for either he will hate the one, and love the other; or else he will hold to the one, and despise the other. Ye cannot serve God and mammon." Matthew 6:24

The Christian is marked by his convictions, for his own sake, because of others, and for God's sake.
—— "The Hallelujah Chorus" In One Verse, 1996
"For none of us liveth to himself, and no man dieth to himself." Romans 14:7

For God to use our lives, there must be rock-ribbed, unchanging convictions now, tomorrow, and for the rest of our lives.
— Preaching To America, 1999
"Jesus Christ the same yesterday, and to day, and for ever." Hebrews 13:8

Men of convictions are the happiest men.
— It's Dynamite, 1953
"But refuse profane and old wives' fables, and exercise thyself rather unto godliness." 1 Timothy 4:7

Avoid everything that dims your shining, that is questionable, that robs God of His glory, and that keeps others from seeing Christ in you.
— Start the Fire, 1986
"Abstain from all appearance of evil." 1 Thessalonians 5:22

No man ever accomplishes much without strong convictions. Especially is this true in the field of Christian service.
— A Winner Never Quits and A Quitter Never Wins, 1994
"Watch ye, stand fast in the faith, quit you like men, be strong."
1 Corinthians 16:13

Your convictions mean little unless you use them.
— Diamonds In the Rough, 1997
"We having the same spirit of faith, according as it is written, I believed, and therefore have I spoken; we also believe, and therefore speak;"
2 Corinthians 4:13

COURAGE

God gives courage to those who love and serve Him.
— Preaching To America, 1999

"Wait on the LORD: be of good courage, and he shall strengthen thine heart: wait, I say, on the LORD." Psalms 27:14

It is courage that is so sorely needed in our present day society. We do not need the foolhardiness of the marching mobs, but we need the courage that comes from the presence of God.
— Start the Fire, 1986

"Only be thou strong and very courageous, that thou mayest observe to do according to all the law, which Moses my servant commanded thee: turn not from it to the right hand or to the left, that thou mayest prosper whithersoever thou goest." Joshua 1:7

The courage we need comes from the promises of God.
— This Crisis Hour, 1991

For with God nothing shall be impossible." Luke 1:37

Of all our needs, this to me is the greatest — courageous, stalwart men.
— The Big 90, 1999

"Watch ye, stand fast in the faith, quit you like men, be strong."
1 Corinthians 16:13

Weakness and cowardice in the Christian always hurt the cause of Christ, while courage glorifies God. Even the lost world expects Christians to exhibit courage in the trying hours.
— Are You Tired of Living? 1945, renewed in 1986

"Have not I commanded thee? Be strong and of a good courage; be not afraid, neither be thou dismayed: for the LORD thy God is with thee whithersoever thou goest." Joshua 1:9

The greatest stories in the world are the accounts of Christian courage; courage to stand true to Christ even in the face of danger.
— Are You Tired of Living? 1945, renewed in 1986

"If the LORD be God, follow him: but if Baal, then follow him. And the people answered him not a word." 1 Kings 18:21

The fighting heart keeps one moving forward despite circumstances, when all is lost — job, friends, and family - and when people declare it can't be done.
— A Winner Never Quits and A Quitter Never Wins, 1994

"Fight the good fight of faith, lay hold on eternal life, whereunto thou art also called, and hast professed a good profession before many witnesses." 1 Timothy 6:12

CROSS, THE

The cross is the message the world needs to hear. The Christ of the cross is the only Saviour for lost men.
— The Gold Mine, 1996

"For the preaching of the cross is to them that perish foolishness; but unto us which are saved it is the power of God." 1 Corinthians 1:18

The cross presented a two-fold symbol: first, the symbol of Rome's stern domination; and second, the symbol of ultimate degradation to which a human being could be condemned.
— *"The Hallelujah Chorus" In One Verse, 1996*
"Looking unto Jesus the author and finisher of our faith; who for the joy that was set before him endured the cross, despising the shame, and is set down at the right hand of the throne of God." Hebrews 12:2

The story of the cross begins in Genesis and extends throughout the Word of God.
— *"The Hallelujah Chorus" In One Verse, 1996*
"And all that dwell upon the earth shall worship him, whose names are not written in the book of life of the Lamb slain from the foundation of the world." Revelation 13:8

A familiar sight for Lee Roberson audiences.

Dr. Lee Roberson is one the most unique and effective ministers of the gospel in the twentieth century. He is a compassionate minister, consistent soulwinner, and a staunch proclaimer of God's inerrant Word. He modeled effective ministry to his church over more than four decades. This book of carefully selected quotations from Dr. Roberson's ministry will bless and challenge every reader. I encourage you to take advantage of the opportunity to read from the wit and wisdom of this remarkable man.

- James T. Draper, Jr., President of LifeWay Christian Resources, past President, Southern Baptist Convention

D

DEATH

Don't laugh at death! Death is certain — if Christ tarries His coming. No really thoughtful person will speak lightly of death.
—— Ten Thousand Tears, 1980
"And as it is appointed unto men once to die, but after this the judgment:" Hebrews 9:27

DECISIONS

The decisions of this life settle eternity.
—— Fireworks Don't Last, 1982
"Verily, verily, I say unto you, If a man keep my saying, he shall never see death." John 8:51

There are decisions made in a single day which will blight and damn for eternity.
—— Are You Tired of Living? 1945, renewed in 1986
"That they all might be damned who believed not the truth, but had pleasure in unrighteousness." 2 Thessalonians 2:12

The indecisive life is a failure.
—— Two Dogs and Peace of Mind, 1974
"How long halt ye between two opinions? if the LORD be God, follow him: but if Baal, then follow him." 1 Kings 18:21

DEDICATION

I want Christ to frame my life, direct my life and fill my life.
— The Key To Victorious Living, 1978
"For even hereunto were ye called: because Christ also suffered for us, leaving us an example, that ye should follow his steps:" 1 Peter 2:21

We push Christ back into the shadows of our lives. We get annoyed when Christ gets into our plans and makes demands of us.
— "The Hallelujah Chorus" In One Verse, 1996
"Wherefore I was grieved with that generation, and said, They do always err in their heart; and they have not known my ways." Hebrews 3:10

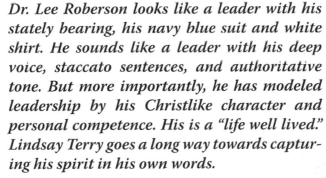

Dr. Lee Roberson looks like a leader with his stately bearing, his navy blue suit and white shirt. He sounds like a leader with his deep voice, staccato sentences, and authoritative tone. But more importantly, he has modeled leadership by his Christlike character and personal competence. His is a "life well lived." Lindsay Terry goes a long way towards capturing his spirit in his own words.

- Bill Monroe, President, Baptist Bible Fellowship International, Pastor, Florence Baptist Temple, Florence, South Carolina

DEFEAT

It is a hard thing for anyone to be defeated without that defeat touching others. Defeat is more contagious than victory.
— "The Hallelujah Chorus" In One Verse, 1996
"Even as I please all men in all things, not seeking mine own profit, but the profit of many, that they may be saved." 1 Corinthians 10:33

DETERMINATION

It is almost impossible to stop a determined Christian. He just puts his head down and says, "This is it. God has called me. He fires on and does the job."
— Fireworks Don't Last, 1982
"Brethren, I count not myself to have apprehended: but this one thing I do, forgetting those things which are behind, and reaching forth unto those things which are before, I press toward the mark for the prize of the high calling of God in Christ Jesus." Philippians 3:13,14

DEVOTION

Meditation is solemn thinking! How this is needed today! We need to do some thinking: What is right? What is wrong? What am I accomplishing? Am I glorifying God? Is my life counting for the most?
— Two Dogs and Peace Of Mind, 1974
"My hands also will I lift up unto thy commandments, which I have loved; and I will meditate in thy statutes." Psalms 119:48

DIE DAILY

Die daily in order to honor Christ, to have peace and contentment, and to bring forth fruit.
— *Preaching To America, 1999*
"Likewise reckon ye also yourselves to be dead indeed unto sin, but alive unto God through Jesus Christ our Lord." Romans 6:11

DEITY OF CHRIST

Let the skeptics and infidels believe what they will, let nothing shake you from the fact that Christ by many infallible proofs showed Himself to be the divine Son of God.
— *Are You Tired Of Living, 1945*
"But ye denied the Holy One and the Just, and desired a murderer to be granted unto you; And killed the Prince of life, whom God hath raised from the dead; whereof we are witnesses."Acts 3:14-15

DISOBEDIENCE

Let me give a warning — some people continue in disobedience so much until they lose their consciousness of their disobedience.
— *The King's Water Boy*
"Holding faith, and a good conscience; which some having put away concerning faith have made shipwreck:" 1 Timothy 1:19

DOUBT

Doubting hearts are cold hearts.
— *Touching Heaven, 1991*
"Then he said unto them, O fools, and slow of heart to believe all that the prophets have spoken: Ought not Christ to have suffered these things, and to enter into his glory?" Luke 24:25-26

Lee Roberson has been a leader among leaders. A Caleb for our generation. Those of us who were privileged to sit under his leadership as students at Tennessee Temple University were forever marked by his teaching, his preaching, and his example. He personified vision, faithfulness, evangelism, and a positive spirit. Dr. Roberson is quick to give His Lord all of the glory, and so do we.

- Paul Dixon, Chancellor, Cedarville University, Cedarville, Ohio

E

ENCOURAGEMENT

Christ is interested in defeated people. The great compassionate Friend is ready to speak words of encouragement and cheer to you in the hour of defeat.
— "The Hallelujah Chorus" In One Verse, 1996
"Come unto me, all ye that labour and are heavy laden, and I will give you rest."
Matthew 11:28

ETERNAL THINGS

The soul cannot be satisfied with temporal things. It cannot be satisfied with the world, for the soul is bigger and more enduring than all the things of this world.
— The King's Water Boy
"And be not conformed to this world: but be ye transformed by the renewing of your mind, that ye may prove what is that good, and acceptable, and perfect, will of God." Romans 12:2

EVANGELISM

Some of Jesus' greatest utterances were to individuals. His healing and evangelistic ministry was one-on-one.
— "The Hallelujah Chorus" In One Verse, 1996
"And Jesus answered and said, Suffer ye thus far. And he touched his ear, and healed him." Luke 22:51 "And he said unto them, Go ye into all the world, and preach the gospel to every creature." Mark 16:15

A moment of quiet reflection.

During the course of a lifetime, one is indeed fortunate to encounter that special person whose impact is strong enough to be life changing. That is the type of person Dr. Lee Roberson has been during his unusual ministry. Over the years of preaching around the world, God has given Dr. Roberson the gift of seeing and saying things no one else was observing or proclaiming. He can identify the essence of a truth and express it in a way to impact the heart.

For Christians in all walks of life, who want to reach the maximum of your potential in serving Jesus Christ, absorb these statements from a man used to touch his generation.

- David Bouler, Chancellor, Tennessee Temple University and Pastor, Highland Park Baptist Church, Chattanooga, Tennessee

F

FAILURE

This is our danger. We are busy with this and that and fail to lay hold upon the riches of God.
— "The Hallelujah Chorus" In One Verse, 1996

"In whom we have redemption through his blood, the forgiveness of sins, according to the riches of his grace;" Ephesians 1:7

There are two big failures in our nation: failure in the home and failure in the church.
— "The Hallelujah Chorus" In One Verse, 1996

"That ye may be blameless and harmless, the sons of God, without rebuke, in the midst of a crooked and perverse nation, among whom ye shine as lights in the world;" Philippians 2:15

FAITH

Build your faith on God's Word, God's past experience with you, and God's work for others.
— This Crisis Hour, 1991

"So then faith cometh by hearing, and hearing by the word of God." Romans 10:17

By faith I am ready to experience death.
— "The Hallelujah Chorus" In One Verse, 1996

"We are confident, I say, and willing rather to be absent from the body, and to be present with the Lord." 2 Corinthians 5:8

Faith gives peace of heart in the midst of a storm.
— Fireworks Don't Last, 1982

"Peace I leave with you, my peace I give unto you: not as the world giveth, give I unto you. Let not your heart be troubled, neither let it be afraid." John 14:27

The greatest faith is born in the hour of despair. When we can see no hope and no way out, then faith rises and brings the victory.
— The Faith That Moves Mountains, 1984
"Remembering without ceasing your work of faith, and labour of love, and patience of hope in our Lord Jesus Christ, in the sight of God and our Father;" 1 Thessalonians 1:3

Unbelief is infectious. Don't let yourself be influenced by the faithless.
— The Faith That Moves Mountains, 1984
"For what if some did not believe? shall their unbelief make the faith of God without effect?" Romans 3:3

See Elijah's childlike faith in God. He accepted the Word of God without question, did not flinch in the presence of the severest demands, did not stagger by apparent improbabilities, was prompt in obedience, and enjoyed the fulfillment of the divine promise.
— Compassion Unlimited
"So he went and did according unto the word of the LORD" 1 Kings 17:5

Please notice that if Satan did not hesitate to work upon the Son of God, then he will not hesitate to try to defeat your life.
— Start the Fire, 1986
"But if our gospel be hid, it is hid to them that are lost: In whom the god of this world hath blinded the minds of them which believe not, lest the light of the glorious gospel of Christ, who is the image of God, should shine unto them." 2 Corinthians 4:3-4

Faith makes life exciting, flexible, progressive, unselfish, and victorious.
— The Faith That Moves Mountains, 1984
"For whatsoever is born of God overcometh the world: and this is the victory that overcometh the world, even our faith." 1 John 5:4

The force of faith in the life of the apostle Paul: It saved him, sent him, and sustained him.
— A Winner Never Quits and A Quitter Never Wins, 1994
"And the Lord shall deliver me from every evil work, and will preserve me unto his heavenly kingdom: to whom be glory for ever and ever. Amen." 2 Timothy 4:18

The fearful, trembling person indicates that he is looking too much to himself and depending too much upon human power, and not enough on divine resources.
— "The Hallelujah Chorus" In One Verse, 1996
"Fight the good fight of faith, lay hold on eternal life, whereunto thou art also called, and hast professed a good profession before many witnesses." 1 Timothy 6:12

Faith in God is also a builder of character.
— "The Hallelujah Chorus" In One Verse, 1996
"If ye continue in the faith grounded and settled, and be not moved away from the hope of the gospel, which ye have heard, and which was preached to every creature which is under heaven; whereof I Paul am made a minister;" Colossians 1:23

Lack of faith is a stumbling block to others. When we are faithless, others are affected.
— The Faith That Moves Mountains, 1984
"But ye are departed out of the way; ye have caused many to stumble at the law; ye have corrupted the covenant of Levi, saith the LORD of hosts." Malachi 2:8

You can increase your faith by obedience to God's every command, by an appreciation of His love and presence, and by attempting the impossible.
—— The Faith That Moves Mountains, 1984
"And the apostles said unto the Lord, Increase our faith. And the Lord said, If ye had faith as a grain of mustard seed, ye might say unto this sycamine tree, Be thou plucked up by the root, and be thou planted in the sea; and it should obey you." Luke 17:6

You build a daring, dynamic faith by the Word of God, by worship, and by courageous actions.
—— The Faith That Moves Mountains, 1984
"Jesus said unto him, If thou canst believe, all things are possible to him that believeth." Mark 9:23

Faith in God makes difficulties look small and imparts strength for the toughest battles.
—— People: a Book About Bible People, 1983
"I can do all things through Christ which strengtheneth me." Philippians 4:13

Faith is resting and relying on the Lord for the fulfillment of all His promises.
—— The Faith That Moves Mountains, 1984
"I am crucified with Christ: nevertheless I live; yet not I, but Christ liveth in me: and the life which I now live in the flesh I live by the faith of the Son of God, who loved me, and gave himself for me." Galatians 2:20

For yours to be a happy faith, do the following: Depend on God to stand with you, depend on God to provide, and depend on God to strengthen you.
—— The Faith That Moves Mountains, 1984
"I will say of the LORD, He is my refuge and my fortress: my God; in him will I trust." Psalms 91:2

Constantly we look into the Word of God, then go out to walk the way of faith. We do not need to look to tomorrow but receive the promises as manna for each day.
—— The Faith That Moves Mountains, 1984
"So then faith cometh by hearing, and hearing by the word of God." Romans 10:17

Faith can add peace, courage, and adventure to your life.
—— The Faith That Moves Mountains, 1984
"Be careful for nothing; but in every thing by prayer and supplication with thanksgiving let your requests be made known unto God. And the peace of God, which passeth all understanding, shall keep your hearts and minds through Christ Jesus." Philippians 4:6,7

God is glorified by that Christian who refuses to worry.
—— The Faith That Moves Mountains, 1984
"Therefore I say unto you, Take no thought for your life, what ye shall eat, or what ye shall drink; nor yet for your body, what ye shall put on. Is not the life more than meat, and the body than raiment?" Matthew 6:25

The three dimensions of faith are: visible faith, vicarious faith, and victorious faith.
—— The Faith That Moves Mountains, 1984
"For whatsoever is born of God overcometh the world: and this is the victory that overcometh the world, even our faith." 1 John 5:4

True faith is never static! Even the faith of a Christian shut-in can be active and working.
—— The Faith That Moves Mountains, 1984
"But let him ask in faith, nothing wavering. For he that wavereth is like a wave of the sea driven with the wind and tossed." James 1:6

Without faith — telling faith from God which is based on the living and written Word of God — no one can reach the heights of spiritual greatness, or obtain great things from God.
— A Winner Never Quits and A Quitter Never Wins, 1994

"And Jesus said unto them, Because of your unbelief: for verily I say unto you, If ye have faith as a grain of mustard seed, ye shall say unto this mountain, Remove hence to yonder place; and it shall remove; and nothing shall be impossible unto you." Matthew 17:20

Faith sees the invisible
Faith hears the inaudible
Faith believes the incredible
Faith receives the impossible
— The Faith That Moves Mountains, 1984

"And Jesus looking upon them saith, With men it is impossible, but not with God: for with God all things are possible." Mark 10:27

The way to develop or increase your faith is to be obedient to God's every command, be appreciative of His love and presence, and attempt the impossible.
— The Faith That Moves Mountains, 1984

"And he said, The things which are impossible with men are possible with God." Luke 18:27

Faith sings, for faith blasts away doubt and fear. Faith lets the light shine through the darkest clouds. Faith gives a lift to the heavy heart.
— It's Dynamite, 1953

"I am crucified with Christ: nevertheless I live; yet not I, but Christ liveth in me: and the life which I now live in the flesh I live by the faith of the Son of God, who loved me, and gave himself for me." Galatians 2:20

Our entire dependence upon the merits and mediation of the Lord Jesus Christ is our only grounds for any claim for blessings.
—— It's Dynamite, 1953
"If ye shall ask any thing in my name, I will do it." John 14:14

The fighting heart must be right with God, have courage, determination, and devotion.
—— A Winner Never Quits and A Quitter Never Wins, 1994
"Fight the good fight of faith, lay hold on eternal life, whereunto thou art also called, and hast professed a good profession before many witnesses." 1 Timothy 6:12

The world is breeding a kind of tolerance for all religions and heresies until there will be but a few voices raised in the next few years for the old-time faith.
—— The Faith That Moves Mountains, 1984
"Beloved, when I gave all diligence to write unto you of the common salvation, it was needful for me to write unto you, and exhort you that ye should earnestly contend for the faith which was once delivered unto the saints." Jude 1:3

We find examples of faith in men of olden days who did not fail:
In Abel, we have the worship of faith.
In Enoch, the walk of faith.
In Noah, the witness of faith.
In Abraham, we have the wandering of faith.
In Sarah, we have the waiting of faith.
In Moses, we have the work of faith.
—— The Faith That Moves Mountains, 1984
"Now faith is the substance of things hoped for, the evidence of things not seen." Hebrews 11:1

FAITHFULNESS

In this wishy-washy, uncertain day, we should be known for dependability. Homes, businesses, schools, nations, and churches operate on dependability.
— "The Hallelujah Chorus" In One Verse, 1996
"But let him ask in faith, nothing wavering. For he that wavereth is like a wave of the sea driven with the wind and tossed." James 1:6

The characteristic of abiding work must certainly be faithfulness.
— Some Golden Daybreak, 1957
"Be thou faithful unto death, and I will give thee a crown of life." Revelation 2:10

The failure to be faithful will mean the loss of peace of heart, the loss of influence, the loss of joy, and the loss of reward.
— This Crisis Hour, 1991
"Moreover it is required in stewards, that a man be found faithful." 1 Corinthians 4:2

Faithfulness to God will bring down divine blessings beyond anything that this world can know about.
— It's Dynamite, 1953
"By faith Noah, being warned of God of things not seen as yet, moved with fear, prepared an ark to the saving of his house; by the which he condemned the world, and became heir of the righteousness which is by faith." Hebrews 11:7

FEAR

Fear defeats you, destroys your testimony, weakens your life and dishonors God.
— The Faith That Moves Mountains, 1984

"For God hath not given us the spirit of fear; but of power, and of love, and of a sound mind." 2 Timothy 1:7

Fear is a common thing in this day, but fear will be gone in His presence and in His place.
— Ten Thousand Tears, 1980

"Be strong and of a good courage, fear not, nor be afraid of them: for the LORD thy God, he it is that doth go with thee; he will not fail thee, nor forsake thee." Deuteronomy 31:6

Let all things press you to His side.
— Preaching to America, 1999

"The LORD is nigh unto all them that call upon him, to all that call upon him in truth." Psalms 145:18

Leading a graduation exercise at Tennessee Temple University.

Both Lee Roberson, the subject of this book, and Lindsay Terry, the compiler, are personal friends. I visited Lee Roberson at Highland Park Baptist Church in 1969 when I was writing the book, **The Ten Largest Sunday Schools and What Made Them Grow.** *At that time, Dr. Roberson had built the second largest church in the world, and had a vast outreach to over 100 Sunday school chapels in the Greater Chattanooga area.*

I was greatly impressed with his evangelistic zeal and commitment to the fundamentals of the faith. May you read and be inspired by the wit and wisdom of one of the greatest leaders in the past 60 years.

- Elmer Towns, Author, Vice President, Liberty University and Dean, School of Religion

G

GIVING

We must have the compassion that expresses itself in giving and sends us to the lost around us.
—— "The Hallelujah Chorus" In One Verse, 1996

"But when he saw the multitudes, he was moved with compassion on them, because they fainted, and were scattered abroad, as sheep having no shepherd." Matthew 9:36

Give in the light of Scriptural happenings: the anguish of Gethsemane, the light of Calvary, the empty tomb, the great commission, the Day of Pentecost, and the second coming of Jesus Christ.
—— The Key To a Changed Life, 1978

"Give, and it shall be given unto you; good measure, pressed down, and shaken together, and running over, shall men give into your bosom. For with the same measure that ye mete withal it shall be measured to you again." Luke 6:38

GODLINESS

What identifies a man of God? His disciplined life, his hatred for sin and error, and his activity in service.
—— The Big 90, 1999

"I must work the works of him that sent me, while it is day: the night cometh, when no man can work." John 9:4

GOD'S LOVE

The love of God does not negate the fact of the judgment of God.
—— "The Hallelujah Chorus" In One Verse, 1996

"For the wages of sin is death; but the gift of God is eternal life through Jesus Christ our Lord." Romans 6:23

Jesus revealed God's love by His actions, His words, His prayers, and His death.

— "The Hallelujah Chorus" In One Verse, 1996

"Herein is love, not that we loved God, but that he loved us, and sent his Son to be the propitiation for our sins." 1 John 4:10

You have missed much of the message of our God if you miss the consciousness of His love for you!

— Touching Heaven, 1991

"The LORD hath appeared of old unto me, saying, Yea, I have loved thee with an everlasting love: therefore with lovingkindness have I drawn thee." Jeremiah 31:3

GOD'S POWER

Some people have the power but not the willingness to help. Others have the willingness but not the power. God has both.

— The Faith That Moves Mountains, 1984

"I can do all things through Christ which strengtheneth me." Philippians 4:13

As an eighteen-year-old I enrolled in Tennessee Temple University. I remember the first time I saw Dr. Roberson — the distinguished gray hair, the big voice, and his commanding presence. I will always be thankful for the great impact he had on my life and ministry. He always encouraged us to stay faithful and impressed on us that "winners never quit."

- Larry Black, Minister of Music Emeritus, First Baptist Church, Jackson, Mississippi

Beaten men emphasize their weakness instead of God's strength.
— Compassion Unlimited
"And Jesus came and spake unto them, saying, All power is given unto me in heaven and in earth." Matthew 28:18

The honest, upright, consistent Christian life is endued with power from on high.
— It's Dynamite, 1953
"All thy works shall praise thee, O LORD; and thy saints shall bless thee. They shall speak of the glory of thy kingdom, and talk of thy power;" Psalms 145:10,11

GOD'S PRESENCE

Whether diseased, or dead, or despised — God is ready to manifest Himself to us. He is nearer then hands or feet.
— The Witness Book, 1965
"As I was with Moses, so I will be with thee: I will not fail thee, nor forsake thee." Joshua 1:5

GOD'S PROMISES

To find beauty in the sad hours will cost you something. You will need hours of fellowship with God. You will need to have unlimited confidence in His promises.
— Two Dogs and Peace of Mind, 1974
"For all the promises of God in him are yea, and in him Amen, unto the glory of God by us." 2 Corinthians 1:20

GOD'S VOICE

God may not speak in the strong wind, the earthquake, or the fire; but after all of those things will come the still small voice.
—— Are You Tired of Living? 1945, renewed in 1986
"Speak, LORD; for thy servant heareth." 1 Samuel 3:9

GOD'S WILL

The right medicine for America is a surrender to the will of God.
—— Preaching to America, 1999
"Blessed is the nation whose God is the LORD; and the people whom he hath chosen for his own inheritance." Psalms 33:12

To continue in God's will means to keep the goal before your eyes.
—— This Crisis Hour, 1991
"Furthermore then we beseech you, brethren, and exhort you by the Lord Jesus, that as ye have received of us how ye ought to walk and to please God, so ye would abound more and more." 1 Thessalonians 4:1

The man who does not see God leading him will soon be out of harmony with God.
—— 7 Life Changing Statements, 1972
"For as many as are led by the Spirit of God, they are the sons of God." Romans 8:14

God has a will for every Christian, and it is a Christian's part to know His will and to do it.
— The Key to Victorious Living, 1978

"For this cause we also, since the day we heard it, do not cease to pray for you, and to desire that ye might be filled with the knowledge of his will in all wisdom and spiritual understanding;" Colossians 1:9

GROWTH

When one gets saved, the only way of safety is to cut loose from the world and all entangling alliances. Make a clean break with the past. Face it and march forward with Him.
— A Winner Never Quits and A Quitter Never Wins, 1994

"Therefore if any man be in Christ, he is a new creature: old things are passed away; behold, all things are become new." 2 Corinthians 5:17

GUIDANCE

The voice we must hear is the voice of God. He speaks by His Word, by His servants, and through the indwelling Holy Spirit.
— A Winner Never Quits and A Quitter Never Wins, 1994

"Howbeit when he, the Spirit of truth, is come, he will guide you into all truth: for he shall not speak of himself; but whatsoever he shall hear, that shall he speak: and he will shew you things to come." John 16:13

Lots of work to do in the office.

Dr. Lee Roberson is one of the greatest men I know. I have for years felt a kinship to him and am honored to call him my friend. Dr. Roberson has literally touched the lives of multiplied thousands of people through the schools he has founded, the great church he has pastored, the books he has written, and his preaching across America. I have spent hours with him and have always come away feeling he had my best interest at heart. May God give America many more men like Lee Roberson.

- Tom Malone, Sr., President and Founder, Midwestern Baptist College, Pontiac, Michigan

H

HAPPINESS

The life without a definite purpose and aim is bound to be one of unhappiness. If you want happiness in your life, get something to do and stick to it.

— Are You Tired of Living? 1945, renewed in 1986

"I must work the works of him that sent me, while it is day: the night cometh, when no man can work." John 9:4

HARDSHIPS

Our difficulties, our heartaches, and our failures do three things for us — they toughen us, teach us, and tender us.

— The University of Hard Knocks, 1960

"My grace is sufficient for thee: for my strength is made perfect in weakness. Most gladly therefore will I rather glory in my infirmities, that the power of Christ may rest upon me." 2 Corinthians 12:9

HEART, THE

We often speak of revivals beginning in churches, but we are conscious of the fact that the revivals actually start in the individual heart and spreads from one heart to another.

— The King's Water Boy

"But as it is written, Eye hath not seen, nor ear heard, neither have entered into the heart of man, the things which God hath prepared for them that love him." 1 Corinthians 2:9

HEAVEN

There has been a rumor abroad in the human race for centuries that entrance into heaven could be obtained by presentation of good works.
— This Crisis Hour, 1991

"For by grace are ye saved through faith; and that not of yourselves: it is the gift of God: Not of works, lest any man should boast." Ephesians 2:8-9

Heaven is so glorious that God uses negatives to describe it. No sin, no curse, no sorrow, no pain, no separation.
— Some Golden Daybreak, 1957

"And they shall see his face; and his name shall be in their foreheads. And there shall be no night there; and they need no candle, neither light of the sun; for the Lord God giveth them light: and they shall reign for ever and ever." Revelation 22:4-5

The fullness of Heaven is in the future. Only a foretaste of Heaven can be had now.
— Are You Tired of Living? 1945

"But as it is written, Eye hath not seen, nor ear heard, neither have entered into the heart of man, the things which God hath prepared for them that love him." 1 Corinthians 2:9

So you can see that Heaven is not a vague, disembodied state from the saved dead. It is real. We are going to have real bodies like the body of Christ.
— Death and After? 1954

"In my Father's house are many mansions: if it were not so, I would have told you. I go to prepare a place for you." John 14:2

If Christ is your Saviour, you are as sure of Heaven as if you were there right now.
— Are You Tired of Living? 1945
"For we know that if our earthly house of this tabernacle were dissolved, we have a building of God, an house not made with hands, eternal in the heavens." 2 Corinthians 5:1

Here is the divine specific for heart control:
First, there is faith in the Lord Jesus Christ. Second, there is the assurance that the Father's house will be our heavenly home. Third, there is the realization that the Saviour had done and is doing everything necessary to secure us a welcome there and fit that home for our reception. Fourth, there is the blessed hope that He is coming in person to receive us unto Himself. Fifth, there is the precious promise that we are to be with Him forever.
— The Big 90, 1999
"And if I go and prepare a place for you, I will come again, and receive you unto myself; that where I am, there ye may be also." John 14:3

It is not our business to reign now. In this age we are "fools for Christ's sake." The day of our reigning is still in the future. This will be in the time when Christ comes again and when the saints shall judge the world.
— Mr. Saint and Mr. Sinner Look at the Second Coming of Christ, 1963
"...and they lived and reigned with Christ a thousand years." Revelation 20:4

HOLY SPIRIT

Let us not forget that the filling of the Holy Spirit is for a definite purpose, that we might live victoriously and that we might be good witnesses for our Saviour. His power comes upon us day by day that we might be witnesses of Him.
— People: A Book About Bible People, 1983
"But ye shall receive power, after that the Holy Ghost is come upon you: and ye shall be witnesses unto me both in Jerusalem, and in all Judaea, and in Samaria, and unto the uttermost part of the earth." Acts 1:8

Are you thinking the thoughts of God?
— Two Dogs and Peace of Mind, 1974
"Finally, brethren, whatsoever things are true, whatsoever things are honest, whatsoever things are just, whatsoever things are pure, whatsoever things are lovely, whatsoever things are of good report; if there be any virtue, and if there be any praise, think on these things." Philippians 4:8

The Christian life lacks completeness without an understanding of the Holy Spirit.
— This Crisis Hour, 1991
"He shall glorify me: for he shall receive of mine, and shall shew it unto you." John 16:14

It is impossible to believe that one can be filled with the Holy Spirit unless he is one who prays.
— Preaching to America, 1999
"If ye then, being evil, know how to give good gifts unto your children: how much more shall your heavenly Father give the Holy Spirit to them that ask him?" Luke 11:13

The fullness of the Holy Spirit gives:
Boldness
Facility in speech
Grace to stand in times of persecution
Vision
Love for others
Determination
A reward at the Judgment Seat of Christ
— This Crisis Hour, 1991
"Howbeit when he, the Spirit of truth, is come, he will guide you into all truth: for he shall not speak of himself; but whatsoever he shall hear, that shall he speak: and he will shew you things to come." John 16:13

I have made a thousand mistakes when I did something on my own, but never a single one when I depended upon the Heavenly Father and the Holy Spirit's power.
— Diamonds In the Rough, 1997
"Give me understanding, and I shall keep thy law; yea, I shall observe it with my whole heart." Psalms 119:34

The Holy Spirit guides us by the Bible, by barriers, and by blessings.
— "The Hallelujah Chorus" In One Verse, 1996
"Now when they had gone throughout Phrygia and the region of Galatia, and were forbidden of the Holy Ghost to preach the word in Asia, After they were come to Mysia, they assayed to go into Bithynia: but the Spirit suffered them not." Acts 16:6-7

Life has no abiding splendor unless it is given us by the indwelling Holy Spirit.
— Coming to Chattanooga...Soon, 1980

"In whom ye also trusted, after that ye heard the word of truth, the gospel of your salvation: in whom also after that ye believed, ye were sealed with that holy Spirit of promise," Ephesians 1:13

We fall because we are unwilling to take of the fullness of the Spirit of God.
— The Key To a Changed Life, 1978

"In whom ye also trusted, after that ye heard the word of truth, the gospel of your salvation: in whom also after that ye believed, ye were sealed with that holy Spirit of promise," Ephesians 1:13

In addition to all else the Holy Spirit does for us, He will give us victory in the hour of dying. Someone has said, "Triumphant dying is the Amen to a godly life."
— It's Dynamite, 1953

"For to me to live is Christ, and to die is gain." Philippians 1:21

When the Holy Spirit leads, the following will always be true:
We will always be in the right place.
We will always be on praying ground.
We will always have peace.
— The Big 90, 1999

"For as many as are led by the Spirit of God, they are the sons of God." Romans 8:14

There are seven meaningful works of the Holy Spirit:
"He shall teach you all things." John 14:26
"He shall...bring all things to your remembrance." John 14:26
"He shall testify of me (Jesus)." John 15:26
"He will reprove the world." John 16:8
"He will guide you into all truth." John 16:13
"He will show you things to come." John 16:13
"He shall glorify Me." John 16:14
— *"The Hallelujah Chorus" In One Verse, 1996*

HOME

Locking the Bible outside will destroy the home as sure as you live. If the home is going to stand, there must be a recognition of the teaching of the Bible.
— *Fireworks Don't Last, 1982*
"Thy word have I hid in mine heart, that I might not sin against thee." Psalms 119:11

HUMILITY

When we remain little in our own eyes, we are kept out of the sight of men.
— *Preaching To America, 1999*
"For ye are dead, and your life is hid with Christ in God." Colossians 3:3

Leading a student chapel service in the 1970s in the Chauncey-Goode Auditorium.

Dr. Lee Roberson had two great influences on me. First, I visited his church in 1965 and was greatly impressed with its size, evangelistic outreach, and warm Christian fellowship. Highland Park Baptist Church motivated me to come back and build Thomas Road Baptist Church following the same principles. We became one of the ten largest churches in America.

As we began to grow, Dr. Lee Roberson became a friend of mine. I valued his advice and looked forward to our encouraging conversations. I am thrilled to recommend this book to readers and may each one become as inspired as I was in 1965.

- Jerry Falwell, Chancellor, Liberty University and Pastor, Thomas Road Baptist Church, Lynchburg, Virginia

I

INDIFFERENCE

A casual look around us will reveal the thousands who, though they proclaim they have been saved, are guilty of deadly indifference.
— "The Hallelujah Chorus" In One Verse, 1996
"Is it nothing to you, all ye that pass by?" Lamentations 1:12

There are three things facing us in this hour: The nonchalance of youth, the occupation of adulthood, and the blindness and deafness of age.
— Fireworks Don't Last, 1982
"See then that ye walk circumspectly, not as fools, but as wise, Redeeming the time, because the days are evil." Ephesians 5:15,16

INFLUENCE

I confess to you that I like to keep before me a picture of the Apostle Paul and his faithfulness to strengthen my heart and send me on.
— A Winner Never Quits and A Quitter Never Wins, 1994
"And the Lord shall deliver me from every evil work, and will preserve me unto his heavenly kingdom: to whom be glory for ever and ever. Amen." 2 Timothy 4:18

If your influence is to be correct and to be God-honoring, then that influence must be monitored by the Word of God.
— Two Dogs and Peace of Mind, 1974
"Thy word is a lamp unto my feet, and a light unto my path." Psalms 119:105

Your influence should glorify God. Daily help some-one else and point them to Christ.
— Fireworks Don't Last, 1982

"And daily in the temple, and in every house, they ceased not to teach and preach Jesus Christ." Acts 5:42

Are you somebody's inspiration? You should be. There should be about your life those qualities which would inspire someone to nobler living.
— Two Dogs and Peace of Mind, 1974

"It is good neither to eat flesh, nor to drink wine, nor any thing whereby thy brother stumbleth, or is offended, or is made weak." Romans 14:21

Opening a new building on the TTU campus.

Dr. Lee Roberson, blessed by the Lord with a long life, has stayed on the trail and in the harness longer than any man I've ever known. His love of souls has never diminished. He has never rusted out.

- Bob Jones III, Chancellor, Bob Jones University, Greenville, South Carolina

J

JOY

There are three joys in Christ — the joy of living for Him, the joy of working for Him, and the joy of waiting for Him.
— Fireworks Don't Last, 1982

"But none of these things move me, neither count I my life dear unto myself, so that I might finish my course with joy, and the ministry, which I have received of the Lord Jesus, to testify the gospel of the grace of God." Acts 20:24

Before you can have God's best, you must let Him show you what the unclean is which has choked your spiritual vitality. There must be a surrender of everything.
— Preaching To America, 1999

"If we confess our sins, he is faithful and just to forgive us our sins, and to cleanse us from all unrighteousness." 1 John 1:9

Men may build what they feel is a good life, and then find that it is nothing. Too often the attainments bring little joy because of that which happens in the hour of fruition.
— Ten Thousand Tears, 1980

"The fashion of this world passeth away." 1 Corinthians 7:31

JUDGMENT

The fact of judgment is accepted by all people. We are going to be judged!
— Mr. Saint and Mr. Sinner Look at the Second Coming, 1963

"For we must all appear before the judgment seat of Christ; that every one may receive the things done in his body, according to that he hath done, whether it be good or bad." 2 Corinthians 5:10

Dr. Roberson with long-time associate Dr. J. R. Faulkner.

Lee Roberson is one of the most amazing men I have ever known. The contribution that he has made to the cause of Christ and to the lives of so many is literally beyond description. Thankfully, however, Lindsay Terry has gone to the trouble to pull together some of the wonderful insights from the incredible years of preaching, teaching, and writing that Dr. Roberson has pursued. Now we can all sit at his feet and learn.

- Paige Patterson, President, Southwestern Baptist Theological Seminary, Fort Worth, Texas

L

LEADERSHIP

It is sensible to say that for one to live successfully and to be a leader of others, he must plan the way that he himself is going.
— Compassion Unlimited
"Prepare thy work without, and make it fit for thyself in the field; and afterwards build thine house." Proverbs 24:27

I believe that leadership can be developed. Some would say that "leaders are born." This is only partially true. A leader has certain characteristics — most of them can be acquired by diligent thought and effort.
— Compassion Unlimited
"Not because we have not power, but to make ourselves an ensample unto you to follow us." 2 Thessalonians 3:7-9

Everything rises and falls on leadership.
(Although many have contributed this quote to him, Dr. Roberson does not take credit for the originality of it. He does, however, remember that he has used it for more than 55 years.)
— A winner Never Quits and A Quitter Never Wins, 1994
"Those things, which ye have both learned, and received, and heard, and seen in me, do: and the God of peace shall be with you." Philippians 4:9

A great Christian leader is filled with the Spirit of God, knows the Bible, has strong convictions, is concerned for others, and is submissive to the will of God.
— A Winner Never Quits and A Quitter Never Wins, 1994
"Therefore, my beloved brethren, be ye stedfast, unmoveable, always abounding in the work of the Lord, forasmuch as ye know that your labour is not in vain in the Lord." 1 Corinthians 15:58

A great Christian leader gives attention to:
Salvation
Dedication
Diplomacy
Determination
Death
Direction
— A Winner Never Quits and A Quitter Never Wins, 1994
"And as it is appointed unto men once to die, but after this the judgment."
Hebrews 9:27

LIFE

The Christian's present life is a time of trouble,
sorrow, change, disappointment, opportunity, prep-
aration, and expression.
— Fireworks Don't Last, 1982
"Man that is born of a woman is of few days, and full of trouble." Job 14:1

LIFE IN CHRIST

The grandest fact of the present is that Jesus Christ,
the Lord of Glory, was made in the likeness of men
and became obedient unto death in order that we
might be saved.
— Some Golden Daybreak, 1957
"And the Word was made flesh, and dwelt among us, (and we beheld his
glory, the glory as of the only begotten of the Father,) full of grace and truth."
John 1:14

Righteousness is still the greatest weapon.
— The Gold Mine, 1996

"And be found in him, not having mine own righteousness, which is of the law, but that which is through the faith of Christ, the righteousness which is of God by faith:" Philippians 3:9

The most important fact of the present is that Jesus is now seated at God's right hand, making intercession for us.
— Some Golden Daybreak, 1957

"Wherefore he is able also to save them to the uttermost that come unto God by him, seeing he ever liveth to make intercession for them." Hebrews 7:25

The greatest event of the future is that this same Lord Jesus shall come again and receive us unto Himself.
— Some Golden Daybreak, 1957

"And if I go and prepare a place for you, I will come again, and receive you unto myself; that where I am, there ye may be also." John 14:3

It is good for us to know what is small and what is large. Magnify the things that are important and minimize the small things in life.
— Diamonds In the Rough, 1997

"For our light affliction, which is but for a moment, worketh for us a far more exceeding and eternal weight of glory;" 2 Corinthians 4:17

I say to you, keep your eyes upon Jesus. It matters not how difficult, how trying, how destitute seems the way. Light will come upon you when Christ looks down.
— The Gold Mine, 1996

"And your feet shod with the preparation of the gospel of peace;" Ephesians 6:15

Life has purpose only when Christ is leading us. Fortunate is he who looks to the leadership of the Lord and says, "Where He leads me, I will follow."
— The Gold Mine, 1996

"He restoreth my soul: he leadeth me in the paths of righteousness for his name's sake." Psalms 23:3

LITTLE PEOPLE

A man can be little without effort, but no man can be big without effort. Little people are hypocritical, selfish, cowardly, and critical.
— This Crisis Hour, 1991

"Recompense to no man evil for evil. Provide things honest in the sight of all men." Romans 12:17

LOOKING BACK

Don't dwell on past accomplishments:
Keep looking forward.
Keep looking upward.
Keep looking outward.
Keep looking inward.
— Compassion Unlimited

"Brethren, I count not myself to have apprehended: but this one thing I do, forgetting those things which are behind, and reaching forth unto those things which are before, I press toward the mark for the prize of the high calling of God in Christ Jesus." Philippians 3:13-14

LOST

Lost — a word of hopelessness, suffering, shame, and challenge.
—— A Winner Never Quits and A Quitter Never Wins, 1994

"That at that time ye were without Christ, being aliens from the commonwealth of Israel, and strangers from the covenants of promise, having no hope, and without God in the world." Ephesians 2:12

LOVE, GOD'S

No one who knows Christ would ever think of the Master in terms of harshness or unkindness. Christ the Savior expressed to the world the love of God.
—— This Crisis Hour, 1991

"For God so loved the world, that he gave his only begotten Son, that whosoever believeth in him should not perish, but have everlasting life." John 3:16

No work will abide which is not done in love and unselfishness.
—— Some Golden Daybreak, 1957

"Keep yourselves in the love of God, looking for the mercy of our Lord Jesus Christ unto eternal life." Jude 1:21

The love of God is condescending as it reaches down to the lowest sinner. We rejoice that He turns away from no one.
—— "The Hallelujah Chorus" In One Verse, 1996

"But God commendeth his love toward us, in that, while we were yet sinners, Christ died for us." Romans 5:8

LOVE

Love and faithful service are bound together. If you love the Son of God, you will surely serve Him.

— The Gold Mine, 1996

"If ye love me, keep my commandments." John 14:15

Love is essential to Christlikeness, growth in grace, and Christian works.

— Preaching to America, 1999

"But I say unto you, Love your enemies, bless them that curse you, do good to them that hate you, and pray for them which despitefully use you, and persecute you;" Matthew 5:44

We must be so loving in action, in attitude, and in our deeds that men and women will be pointed to our loving Saviour.

— The Gold Mine, 1996

"Charity suffereth long, and is kind; charity envieth not; charity vaunteth not itself, is not puffed up," 1 Corinthians 13:4

Dr. Roberson sitting on the platform during a service at Highland Park Baptist Church. Deeply involved in the activities of the moment.

Eternity will fully reveal the scope and depth of Dr. Lee Roberson's years of faithful ministry, reaching worldwide through many areas of ministry. The extension of his life is seen in the ministries of the graduates of Tennessee Temple University, both through pastors and missionaries. We remember so well when Dr. Roberson would say with full conviction, "Be faithful."

- Jack and Kay Arthur, Precept Ministries International

MEDIOCRITY

*For Christians to be saved from the sin of mediocrity
they should:*
Believe the Bible and rest on God's promises.
Remember that God has never failed.
Believe that God is concerned about you.
Be optimistic and cheerful no matter the problem.
Launch out into the deep.
—— The Faith That Removes Mountains, 1984

"But without faith it is impossible to please him: for he that cometh to God must believe that he is, and that he is a rewarder of them that diligently seek him." Hebrews 11:6

MINISTRY

God uses the man...
who has but one great purpose in life,
who has removed every hindrance,
who has placed himself absolutely at God's disposal,
who is a student of the Word of God,
who has a vital, living message for a lost world,
who is a man of faith,
who walks under the anointing of the Holy Spirit.
—— The Big 90, 1999

"Only Luke is with me. Take Mark, and bring him with thee: for he is profitable to me for the ministry." 2 Timothy 4:11

*There are too many people who are saying nice things
about Jesus and doing nothing for Him.*
—— This Crisis Hour, 1991

"And why call ye me, Lord, Lord, and do not the things which I say?" Luke 6:46

MIRACLES

Miracles happen today when Jesus passes by and men recognize His presence. The commonplace become extraordinary and life takes on new meaning.
— "The Hallelujah Chorus" In One Verse, 1996
"Therefore if any man be in Christ, he is a new creature: old things are passed away; behold, all things are become new." 2 Corinthians 5:17

MISSIONS

No man is Christlike who is not missionary.
— "The Hallelujah Chorus" In One Verse, 1996
"Go ye therefore, and teach all nations, baptizing them in the name of the Father, and of the Son, and of the Holy Ghost:" Matthew 28:19

Missions will make the church courageous, consecrated, and compassionate.
— Start the Fire, 1986
"Now when they saw the boldness of Peter and John, and perceived that they were unlearned and ignorant men, they marvelled; and they took knowledge of them, that they had been with Jesus." Acts 4:13

There are four reason why I believe in missions:
The eternity of the soul,
The veracity of Christ,
The destiny of the damned, and
The uncertainty of life
— Start the Fire, 1986
"For though I preach the gospel, I have nothing to glory of: for necessity is laid upon me; yea, woe is unto me, if I preach not the gospel!" 1 Corinthians 9:16

MONEY

Materialism is the god of American people.
— This Crisis Hour, 1991

"For the love of money is the root of all evil: which while some coveted after, they have erred from the faith, and pierced themselves through with many sorrows." 1 Timothy 6:10

There are people now driving themselves into premature graves because of the love of money. Ambition has seized their hearts, and they can see nothing else.
— Diamonds In the Rough, 1997

"Ye ask, and receive not, because ye ask amiss, that ye may consume it upon your lusts." James 4:3

MURMURING

A murmurer is one who is short of sight. He is confined to a small space in which he moves.
— Two Dogs and Peace of Mind, 1974

"Do all things without murmurings and disputings:" Philippians 2:14

MUSIC

Sing with the hosts of the redeemed, not a lament for lost things, but the song of deliverance. Weep no more in a strange land where sin has taken you, but return to Christ that your joy may be full as it was in the days of old.
— Are You Tired of Living? 1945

"While I live will I praise the LORD: I will sing praises unto my God while I have any being." Psalms 146:2

God wants us to sing!
— This Crisis Hour, 1991

"For ye were sometimes darkness, but now are ye light in the Lord: walk as children of light:" Ephesians 5:8

The singing of Christ! He was singing as He faced Calvary. You can sing as you face your heartaches, too. You can sing as you face the problems of life, the weaknesses of the body and the suffering. What a picture to cheer us is the singing Christ!
— The Key To Victorious Living, 1978

"And when they had sung an hymn, they went out into the mount of Olives." Matthew 26:30

God loves music! It is one of His best gifts to men.
— Are You Tired of Living? 1945

"It came even to pass, as the trumpeters and singers were as one, to make one sound to be heard in praising and thanking the LORD; and when they lifted up their voice with the trumpets and cymbals and instruments of musick, and praised the LORD, saying, For he is good; for his mercy endureth for ever: that then the house was filled with a cloud, even the house of the LORD; So that the priests could not stand to minister by reason of the cloud: for the glory of the LORD had filled the house of God." 2 Chronicles 5:13,14

If you can't sing with the lips, you can have a song in your heart — the song of Jesus and His love.
— Are You Tired of Living? 1945

"And be not drunk with wine, wherein is excess; but be filled with the Spirit; Speaking to yourselves in psalms and hymns and spiritual songs, singing and making melody in your heart to the Lord;" Ephesians 5:18-19

Sixty years ago, as a teenage boy, I provided the music for a Bible Conference where Dr. Lee Roberson was the dynamic speaker for the week. Many years later I arrived at his church to conduct a revival crusade. Rexella and I were shocked because this spiritual giant helped us unload all of our electronic equipment for the crusade.

Dr. Roberson's humility and graciousness overwhelmed us. I say with all honesty, that after having been sponsored by 10,000 ministers in mass citywide endeavors, that Dr. Roberson is undoubtedly the godliest man I have ever met. His example has made me want to be more like him and like Christ.

- Jack Van Impe, President, Jack Van Impe Ministries International

N

NEED

This is an ugly, dirty, needy world and the only answer is Jesus Christ. Try anything or anybody you want to. There is only one answer — Christ.
— Fireworks Don't Last, 1982

"Neither is there salvation in any other: for there is none other name under heaven given among men, whereby we must be saved." Acts 4:12

NEW BIRTH

The new birth is profoundly simple. It is profound, for it is God's way. It is simple, for it is for sinful man.
— "The Hallelujah Chorus" In One Verse, 1996

"And as Moses lifted up the serpent in the wilderness, even so must the Son of man be lifted up: That whosoever believeth in him should not perish, but have eternal life. For God so loved the world, that he gave his only begotten Son, that whosoever believeth in him should not perish, but have everlasting life." John 3:14-16

A birthday celebration!

Dr. Lee Roberson came to my Dad's church when I was a young boy. I will never forget the impression that stately man had on me. He was velvet steel. I am so thankful that his legacy is being preserved through this magnificent book.

- David Jeremiah, Senior Pastor, Shadow Mountain Community Church, El Cajon, California, President, Turning Point Ministries

O

OBEDIENCE

We have one directive for our lives and our churches : obedience!
—— "The Hallelujah Chorus" In One Verse, 1996

"Then Peter and the other apostles answered and said, We ought to obey God rather than men." Acts 5:29

The early Christians had trouble on the outside but peace in their hearts, a peace and happiness that came by obedience.
—— The Kings Water Boy

"There is no peace, saith my God, to the wicked." Isaiah 57:21

Obedience to God brings peace of heart.
—— "The Hallelujah Chorus" In One Verse, 1996

"And let the peace of God rule in your hearts, to the which also ye are called in one body; and be ye thankful." Colossians 3:15

Partial obedience in your life will mean weakness. Give your all to Christ.
—— The Gold Mine, 1996

"I beseech you therefore, brethren, by the mercies of God, that ye present your bodies a living sacrifice, holy, acceptable unto God, which is your reasonable service." Romans 12:1

If you search your Bible from cover to cover, you will see that the secret of the noblest lives ever lived in this sinful world was obedience.
—— People: A Book About Bible People, 1983

"And Samuel said, Hath the LORD as great delight in burnt offerings and sacrifices, as in obeying the voice of the LORD? Behold, to obey is better than sacrifice, and to hearken than the fat of rams." 1 Samuel 15:22

There are three attitudes you can take towards your cross: You can refuse to bear it and take the coward's way out. You can take your cross, bear it, and complain about its weight. You can take your cross and bear it in the Spirit of Christ.

— Fireworks Don't Last, 1982

"And he that taketh not his cross, and followeth after me, is not worthy of me." Matthew 10:38

God grant that we should learn the foolishness of disobedience and the joy of obeying.

— Diamonds In the Rough, 1997

"For to this end also did I write, that I might know the proof of you, whether ye be obedient in all things." 2 Corinthians 2:9

OTHERS

A concern for the souls of others should mark our lives.

— "The Hallelujah Chorus" In One Verse, 1996

"He that goeth forth and weepeth, bearing precious seed, shall doubtless come again with rejoicing, bringing his sheaves with him." Psalms 126:6

If you want adventure, try the land of unselfishness.

— The Faith That Moves Mountains, 1984

"We then that are strong ought to bear the infirmities of the weak, and not to please ourselves." Romans 15:1

This gleaning from the wit and wisdom of one of the great spiritual giants of the twentieth century will be a blessing to the public at large and an invaluable tool for preachers and teachers. Dr. Roberson, in his life and ministry, has made an indelible imprint on multiplied thousands of people. Those of us privileged to be trained for the ministry under his leadership were always challenged by his humility, deep convictions, and Christ-like example. I think many people would agree that, what Charles Haddon Spurgeon was to the nineteenth century, Dr. Lee Roberson is to the twentieth century.

- Bill Compton, Bible Scholar, Evangelist, Pastor, Albany Baptist Church, Decatur, Alabama. On one occasion Dr. Roberson agreed that Bill Compton was probably the best preacher who ever graduated from TTU.

P

PEACE

The peace of God is that eternal calm which lies too deep down in the praying soul to be troubled by any external disturbance.
— *"The Hallelujah Chorus" In One Verse, 1996*

"And let the peace of God rule in your hearts, to the which also ye are called in one body; and be ye thankful." Colossians 3:15

You can only know the peace of God by surrender to His will.
— *Disturbing Questions...Solid Answers, 1978*

"But the God of all grace, who hath called us unto his eternal glory by Christ Jesus, after that ye have suffered a while, make you perfect, stablish, strengthen, settle you." 1 Peter 5:10

The life of peace is the life of power.
— *Two Dogs and Peace of Mind, 1974*

"I will hear what God the LORD will speak: for he will speak peace unto his people, and to his saints: but let them not turn again to folly." Psalms 85:8

The word "peace" is a strange and battered word in this day.
— *"The Hallelujah Chorus" In One Verse, 1996*

"And as they thus spake, Jesus himself stood in the midst of them, and saith unto them, Peace be unto you." Luke 24:36

Every heart longs for peace. God is waiting to give us His peace, but disobedience robs us. Disobedience defeats the very thing that we desire.
— *The King's Water Boy*

"Thou wilt keep him in perfect peace, whose mind is stayed on thee: because he trusteth in thee." Isaiah 26:3

In this restless and troubled age, there is a universal longing for peace.
— Ten Thousand Tears, 1980

"Let not your heart be troubled: ye believe in God, believe also in me." John 14:1

Christ is the one with peace to give! He is untroubled by the storms, untroubled by the problems, and He has no shortage of peace.
— The Key To Victorious Living, 1978

"Great peace have they which love thy law: and nothing shall offend them." Psalms 119:165

The best Christians in this world are the ones who have the peace of God within their hearts. It is when we know the peace of God that we can be of real help to others.
— "The Hallelujah Chorus" In One Verse, 1996

"Peace I leave with you, my peace I give unto you: not as the world giveth, give I unto you. Let not your heart be troubled, neither let it be afraid." John 14:27

When your heart is aching only the Great Physician can minister to you.
— Two Dogs and Peace of Mind, 1974

"For he knoweth our frame; he remembereth that we are dust." Psalms 103:14

PERSECUTION

We — the watched ones — are encircled by an unfriendly world. Let us not forget for a single moment that this world is against the Christian. It despises God and the Christian way of life.

— Fireworks Don't Last, 1982

"For I think that God hath set forth us the apostles last, as it were appointed to death: for we are made a spectacle unto the world, and to angels, and to men." 1 Corinthians 4:9

PLIGHT OF MEN

Four words describe the pitiful plight of all people until Jesus takes over: helpless, hopeless, homeless, and godless.

— Are You Tired of Living? 1945

"That at that time ye were without Christ, being aliens from the commonwealth of Israel, and strangers from the covenants of promise, having no hope, and without God in the world:" Ephesians 2:12

POWER

The young person needs power to overcome. Satan will try to pervert the young mind and the new believer.

"Let no man despise thy youth; but be thou an example of the believers, in word, in conversation, in charity, in spirit, in faith, in purity." 1 Timothy 4:12

PRAYER

To know the will of God will involve tarrying and praying.
— This Crisis Hour, 1991

"And, behold, I send the promise of my Father upon you: but tarry ye in the city of Jerusalem, until ye be endued with power from on high." Luke 24:49

The hidden life is essential if we are to have victory before men. We cannot give out unless we have previously taken. There must be times and seasons of prayer and meditation.
— Compassion Unlimited

"But let it be the hidden man of the heart, in that which is not corruptible, even the ornament of a meek and quiet spirit, which is in the sight of God of great price." 1 Peter 3:4

This simple Scripture is the quickest answer to the reason why so many people have so little.
— "The Hallelujah Chorus" In One Verse, 1996

"Ye ask, and receive not, because ye ask amiss, that ye may consume it upon your lusts." James 4:3

God has ordained that you, Christian, touch heaven.
— Fireworks Don't Last, 1982

"Evening, and morning, and at noon, will I pray, and cry aloud: and he shall hear my voice." Psalms 55:17

Some "praying" is just the saying of words, perhaps impressive and beautiful, but just words — but true prayer touches Heaven. When you touch Heaven:

Peace comes to your heart.

New power is yours.

A new solution to the most serious problem is yours.

Loneliness is gone.

Fear is dispelled.

A new vision is given.

A new determination to glorify God is imparted to you.

Prayer is touching Heaven!

— Touching Heaven, 1991

"After this manner therefore pray ye: Our Father which art in heaven..." Matthew 6:9

Prayer must come from the depth of the heart. It cannot be offered in a shallow or hypocritical way.

— Touching Heaven, 1991

"Not as I will, but as thou wilt." Matthew 26:39

Prayer is putting ourselves into God's hands, offering Him our petitions for mercies needed and our thanks for mercies obtained. Prayer embraces invocation, supplication, intercession, and thanksgiving.

— Touching Heaven, 1991

"Be careful for nothing; but in every thing by prayer and supplication with thanksgiving let your requests be made known unto God. And the peace of God, which passeth all understanding, shall keep your hearts and minds through Christ Jesus." Philippians 4:6,7

Praying for others has a two-fold benefit — first, prayer for others lifts the man who prays out of himself and brings to view the glories of life. Second, prayer for others benefits those for whom we pray. So few people have learned the joy of intercessory prayer.
— Start the Fire, 1986

"Confess your faults one to another, and pray one for another, that ye may be healed. The effectual fervent prayer of a righteous man availeth much." James 5:16

The flesh has no interest in prayer.
— The Big 90, 1999

"Praying always with all prayer and supplication in the Spirit, and watching thereunto with all perseverance and supplication for all saints;" Ephesians 6:18

The Bible's prayer promises are not only all-inclusive and encouraging, but they are astonishing.
— It's Dynamite, 1953

"Therefore I say unto you, What things soever ye desire, when ye pray, believe that ye receive them, and ye shall have them." Mark 11:24

Lee Roberson changed the course of my life. When I was a young man I heard him say, "everything rises and falls on leadership." I immediately embarked on what has become a lifelong journey of studying and writing about leadership. You will be blessed and encouraged by Dr. Roberson's wit and wisdom. Who knows, perhaps something he has said will change your life too!

- John C. Maxwell, Author, Speaker and Founder of INJOY

In general, most people believe in prayer, but sadly so few actually pray!
— A Winner Never Quits and A Quitter Never Wins, 1994
"And it came to pass, that, as he was praying in a certain place, when he ceased, one of his disciples said unto him, Lord, teach us to pray, as John also taught his disciples." Luke 11:1

Sincere prayer will always result in facing your sin. If prayer does not bring before your eyes your short-comings and failures, then you are not praying.
— Touching Heaven, 1991
"Create in me a clean heart, O God; and renew a right spirit within me." Psalms 51:10

All prayer is as nothing, less than foolishness, unless we want God's will to be done.
— Touching Heaven, 1991
"...according to the will of God commit the keeping of their souls to him in well doing, as unto a faithful Creator." 1 Peter 4:19

Take the privilege of prayer away from the multitudes today and you would fill every asylum in the country twice over in one month.
— Are You Tired of Living? 1945, renewed in 1986
"Thou wilt keep him in perfect peace, whose mind is stayed on thee: because he trusteth in thee." Isaiah 26:3

We say we like to pray, but we do not pray. We say we need to pray, but we do not pray. We say that prayer is a way out of every problem, but we do not pray.
— People: A Book About Bible People, 1983
"...men ought always to pray, and not to faint;" Luke 18:1

The praying man is watchful, unselfish, prepared, faithful, and grateful.
— Touching Heaven, 1991
"Bless the LORD, O my soul: and all that is within me, bless his holy name."
Psalms 103:1

We are losing time, action, motion and power because we have failed to make contact with God. Because of that, we cannot press forward with diligence and power.
— The Gold Mine, 1996
"Pray without ceasing." 1 Thessalonians 5:17

Prayer is not wedging in a few words of petition between your many daily activities. Prayer must be a major activity of your life.
— Touching Heaven, 1991
"Hear my cry, O God; attend unto my prayer. From the end of the earth will I cry unto thee, when my heart is overwhelmed: lead me to the rock that is higher than I." Psalms 61:1-2

The crushed heart is driven to prayer, finds solace in prayer, and is strengthened in prayer.
— The Big 90, 1999
"Then they took away the stone from the place where the dead was laid. And Jesus lifted up his eyes, and said, Father, I thank thee that thou hast heard me. And I knew that thou hearest me always: but because of the people which stand by I said it, that they may believe that thou hast sent me." John 11:41-42

Disobedient Christians cannot pray effectively.
— The Big 90, 1999
"But your iniquities have separated between you and your God, and your sins have hid his face from you, that he will not hear. For your hands are defiled with blood, and your fingers with iniquity; your lips have spoken lies, your tongue hath muttered perverseness." Isaiah 59:2-3

How we should pray:
Pray secretly in the closet of communion.
Pray watchfully in the alertness of wakefulness.
Pray believingly in the simplicity of faith.
Pray abidingly in the will of God and in Christ.
Pray directly in the pointedness of definite petition.
Pray effectively in the power of the Holy Spirit.
—— Touching Heaven, 1991
"But ye, beloved, building up yourselves on your most holy faith, praying in the Holy Ghost," Jude 1:20

The Bible and history give ample evidence that prayer is work.
—— Touching Heaven, 1991
"Confess your faults one to another, and pray one for another, that ye may be healed. The effectual fervent prayer of a righteous man availeth much." James 5:16

Are you discouraged? Just keep on praying. Do you feel that you face some problems for which you do not have an answer? Just keep on praying. Though you have trouble concentrating on the matter of prayer, just keep on praying.
—— The Key To a Changed Life, 1978
"And he spake a parable unto them to this end, that men ought always to pray, and not to faint;" Luke 18:1

Prayer and power cannot be divorced or separated.
—— Touching Heaven, 1991
"But ye shall receive power, after that the Holy Ghost is come upon you: and ye shall be witnesses unto me both in Jerusalem, and in all Judaea, and in Samaria, and unto the uttermost part of the earth." Acts 1:8

I am not too concerned about how long — it's what you are getting from God, how you are getting through to Him.
— The Key To Victorious Living, 1978
"But thou, when thou prayest, enter into thy closet, and when thou hast shut thy door, pray to thy Father which is in secret; and thy Father which seeth in secret shall reward thee openly." Matthew 6:6

PRIDE

Man worships his own inventiveness.
— Fireworks Don't Last, 1982
"God resisteth the proud, but giveth grace unto the humble." James 4:6

PROBLEMS

Man is helpless to solve his own problems. We can see it around us very clearly.
— Fireworks Don't Last, 1982
"I find then a law, that, when I would do good, evil is present with me." Romans 7:21

PROGRESS

The world's great refuse to let despondency disturb progress.
— Are You Tired of Living? 1945
"But the God of all grace, who hath called us unto His eternal glory by Christ Jesus, after that ye have suffered awhile, make you perfect, stablish, strengthen, settle you." I Peter 5:10

Dr. Lee Roberson personifies leadership like no other pastor, educator, or church leader over the last half century. This book is a must read for every lay person, pastor, Christian worker, and student preparing for ministry. You will learn from one of God's giants.

- Tom Messer, President, Trinity Baptist College, Senior Pastor, Trinity Baptist Church, Jacksonville, Florida

R

REALITY

Most amusements and pastimes are only a miserable escape from reality.
— Fireworks Don't Last, 1982
"He that loveth pleasure shall be a poor man: he that loveth wine and oil shall not be rich." Proverbs 21:17

REJOICING

The world is filled with too many sad things. Tears are in every home, along every highway, in the workplace — nowhere are we free of tears, but in Christ there is rejoicing!
— Diamonds In the Rough, 1997
"Therefore I take pleasure in infirmities, in reproaches, in necessities, in persecutions, in distresses for Christ's sake: for when I am weak, then am I strong." 2 Corinthians 12:10

RESURRECTION

The world of unbelievers takes fiendish delight in ridiculing the life, death, and resurrection of Christ.
— Disturbing Questions...Solid Answers, 1978
"And if Christ be not risen, then is our preaching vain, and your faith is also vain." 1 Corinthians 15:14

REVIVAL

You are just one in the church, but you're important. If you are not right, the revival may fail.
— Preaching to America, 1999

"If we say that we have no sin, we deceive ourselves, and the truth is not in us. If we confess our sins, he is faithful and just to forgive us our sins, and to cleanse us from all unrighteousness." 1 John 1:8-9

Dr. Roberson with his wife of 68 years, Caroline.

I have known Lee Roberson for more than fifty years. He is a great man of God. After these years in the harvest field with Dr. Roberson, I can say like the Holy Scriptures said concerning Barnabas, "He is a good man, and full of the Holy Ghost and of faith." He is one of the patriarchs of the twentieth century.

- John Rawlings, Former Pastor, Landmark Baptist Temple, Cincinnati, Ohio, Director, Rawlings Foundation

S

SALVATION

My friend you may handle the many affairs of this world with ease; you may overcome a thousand temptations and trials and live through dangerous experiences, but if you reject the Lord Jesus Christ, that one sin will damn your soul forever.
— The Gold Mine, 1996
"He that believeth and is baptized shall be saved; but he that believeth not shall be damned." Mark 16:16

You cannot patch up an old life; Christ has to make you a new person. Without Christ, we are broken and hopeless and despairing. When we come to Him, He, by His grace, gives us a new nature, a new life.
— Diamonds In the Rough, 1997
"Having therefore, brethren, boldness to enter into the holiest by the blood of Jesus, By a new and living way, which he hath consecrated for us, through the veil, that is to say, his flesh;" Hebrews 10:19-20

Our whole Bible shouts with a voice of thunder, "One Way Home." And that is the way of salvation by grace through faith in Christ."
— Are You Tired of Living? 1945
"Who his own self bare our sins in his own body on the tree, that we, being dead to sins, should live unto righteousness: by whose stripes ye were healed." 1 Peter 2:24

By one single act of life, you become the possessor of everlasting life.
— Preaching to America, 1999
"Verily, verily, I say unto you, He that believeth on me hath everlasting life." John 6:47

Salvation gives a new objective for life.
— The Witness Book, 1965

"Therefore if any man be in Christ, he is a new creature: old things are passed away; behold, all things are become new." 2 Corinthians 5:17

Overcoming devils, with the mind of Christ, is a comparatively small matter; but to have one's name written in the Lamb's Book of Life is something to rejoice over.
— The Crisis Hour, 1991

"And there shall in no wise enter into it any thing that defileth, neither whatsoever worketh abomination, or maketh a lie: but they which are written in the Lamb's book of life." Revelation 21:27

Our church rolls and the Lamb's Book of Life are not the same. Many names have been added to our church rolls which have never been added to the Lamb's Book of Life.
— Are You Tired of Living? 1945

"For with the heart man believeth unto righteousness; and with the mouth confession is made unto salvation." Romans 10:10

Be careful that you are never rude or thoughtless in your talk of salvation; for salvation was purchased by the blood of the Lord Jesus Christ. He died that you might have life.
— The Gold Mine, 1996

"Take heed therefore unto yourselves, and to all the flock, over the which the Holy Ghost hath made you overseers, to feed the church of God, which he hath purchased with his own blood." Acts 20:28

SECOND COMING

Man dreams of a world of justice and equality. This will never be realized apart from the coming of Jesus.
— Some Golden Daybreak, 1957

"So Christ was once offered to bear the sins of many; and unto them that look for him shall he appear the second time without sin unto salvation." Hebrews 9:28

We cannot know the Bible nor understand the Word of God unless we read it in the light of the return of Jesus Christ.
— Coming to Chattanooga...Soon, 1980

"For this we say unto you by the word of the Lord, that we which are alive and remain unto the coming of the Lord shall not prevent them which are asleep.... Then we which are alive and remain shall be caught up together with them in the clouds, to meet the Lord in the air: and so shall we ever be with the Lord." 1 Thessalonians 4:15-17

"Our Saviour's Coming"
This is the truth that energizes.
This is the truth that illuminates.
This is the truth that comforts.
This is the truth that centers on Christ.
— Ten Thousand Tears, 1980

"Beloved, now are we the sons of God, and it doth not yet appear what we shall be: but we know that, when he shall appear, we shall be like him; for we shall see him as he is." 1 John 3:2

No one can read the Word of God, even lightly, without being impressed with His promised return.
— Ten Thousand Tears, 1980

"Therefore be ye also ready: for in such an hour as ye think not the Son of man cometh." Matthew 24:44

Every morning when we arise we should say to ourselves, "Perhaps today the Lord is coming." Every night we should repeat, "Would I be ready for my Lord's return if He should come before I wake in the morning."

— Ten Thousand Tears, 1980

"Watch ye therefore, and pray always, that ye may be accounted worthy to escape all these things that shall come to pass, and to stand before the Son of man." Luke 21:36

For those who are saved, the Second Coming of Christ is not only a doctrine to study, but it is a truth to rejoice every heart. His coming is "the blessed hope," for God's children.

— Some Golden Daybreak, 1957

"Looking for that blessed hope, and the glorious appearing of the great God and our Saviour Jesus Christ;" Titus 2:13

Dr. Roberson, a man of integrity, loving kindness, and a great passion for winning the lost to Jesus Christ has influenced me and many other Christian leaders over the years of his ministry. Only God will reveal how this man of God influenced my life to become a world missionary and how thousands of people have been won to Jesus Christ through this ministry as a result of our contact with him.

I recommend this book because the wisdom of that man cannot be described but only tasted as I have tasted it personally and have tried to the best of my ability to expand it.

- Spiros Zodhiates, President Emeritus, AMG International

It is exceedingly easy to make a lot of guesses and speculations on matters of prophecy. Many have done so and have likewise brought into disrepute the teaching of the second coming and related events.
—— Some Golden Daybreak, 1957

"Watch therefore: for ye know not what hour your Lord doth come." Matthew 24:42

SELF

Four things come from following self:
Laziness
Disruption of Christian service
False teaching
Fleshly sins
—— A Winner Never Quits and A Quitter Never Wins, 1994

"If a man therefore purge himself from these, he shall be a vessel unto honour, sanctified, and meet for the master's use, and prepared unto every good work." 2 Timothy 2:21

SELFISHNESS

The selfish person is rarely loved. You can cure this by getting a vision of Christ who died for you.
—— "The Hallelujah Chorus" In One Verse, 1996

"But this I say, He which soweth sparingly shall reap also sparingly; and he which soweth bountifully shall reap also bountifully. Every man according as he purposeth in his heart, so let him give; not grudgingly, or of necessity: for God loveth a cheerful giver." 2 Corinthians 9:6-7

Some men are saved by the glorious grace of God and then live on in utter selfishness.
— Are You Tired of Living? 1945
"For all seek their own, not the things which are Jesus Christ's." Philippians 2:21

SEPARATION

Elevation of soul separates one from the crowd.
— "The Hallelujah Chorus" In One Verse, 1996
"I pray not that thou shouldest take them out of the world, but that thou should-est keep them from the evil." John 17:15

SERVICE

God is simply asking for your best in the place given unto you. Your job may be small and often unno-ticed, but if you do your best, your reward is equal to that of the most distinguished hero, whose work is acclaimed by the world.
— Start the Fire, 1986
"But none of these things move me, neither count I my life dear unto myself, so that I might finish my course with joy, and the ministry, which I have received of the Lord Jesus, to testify the gospel of the grace of God." Acts 20:24

There are four characteristics which, if found in our works, will make them to abide.
Is the work done in love?
Is the work done unselfishly?
Is the work done willingly?
Is the work done with an attitude of faithfulness?
— Some Golden Daybreak, 1957

"For though I preach the gospel, I have nothing to glory of: for necessity is laid upon me; yea, woe is unto me, if I preach not the gospel! For if I do this thing willingly, I have a reward: but if against my will, a dispensation of the gospel is committed unto me." 1 Corinthians 9:16-17

SIN

The everyday sins — the sin of evil speech, evil thinking, gossip, laziness, and indifference — these are the little things that keep on eating away at us until we fall.
— The Gold Mine, 1996

"Their feet run to evil, and they make haste to shed innocent blood: their thoughts are thoughts of iniquity; wasting and destruction are in their paths." Isaiah 59:7

When sin is settled, the answer to prayer will come.
— The Big 90, 1999

"If we confess our sins, he is faithful and just to forgive us our sins, and to cleanse us from all unrighteousness." 1 John 1:9

There is a rule for all of us to establish: if there is a doubt about a thing, then we had better turn from it. If there is a question mark, it is usually wrong.
— A Winner Never Quits and A Quitter Never Wins, 1994

"And be not conformed to this world: but be ye transformed by the renewing of your mind, that ye may prove what is that good, and acceptable, and perfect, will of God." Romans 12:2

Your besetting sin is the sin you do not want to be reproved for; the sin you are readiest to defend; the sin that often beclouds your spiritual sky; the sin that makes you doubt your present acceptance with God; the sin you are all the time trying to persuade yourself is an infirmity.
—— Are You Tired Of Living? 1945
"...let us lay aside every weight, and the sin which doth so easily beset us, and let us run with patience the race that is set before us," Hebrews 12:1

There is no sin so prevalent in this day as the sin of indifference. Worldliness is rank, but indifference touches the masses.
—— Touching Heaven, 1991
"Lift up your eyes, and look on the fields; for they are white already to harvest." John 4:35

There are still those who are selling themselves for small prices, men and women who will give away their souls for a small sum.
—— The Gold Mine, 1996
"For what is a man profited, if he shall gain the whole world, and lose his own soul? or what shall a man give in exchange for his soul?" Matthew 16:26

We are now living in the night time of world history. The darkness is about us. There is no spot where Satan's power is not felt.
—— Start the Fire, 1986
"And this is the condemnation, that light is come into the world, and men loved darkness rather than light, because their deeds were evil." John 3:19

The magic tricks of Satan are always at evidence.
— Start the Fire, 1986

"Lest Satan should get an advantage of us: for we are not ignorant of his devices." 2 Corinthians 2:11

The blackest of words could no wise describe fully the vile and deceptive character of Satan. All selfishness originated in the devil and is passed on to us. It does not matter whether the selfishness appears in saints or sinners, it is from Satan.
— Start the Fire, 1986

"For we wrestle not against flesh and blood, but against principalities, against powers, against the rulers of the darkness of this world, against spiritual wickedness in high places." Ephesians 6:12

The sin question has ever been before us. When we are saved, we are saved from the power of sin, but the presence of sin is still around.
— The Big 90, 1999

"Let not sin therefore reign in your mortal body, that ye should obey it in the lusts thereof." Romans 6:12

SINCERITY

A Christian is not one because of using the language of Heaven.

"But grow in grace, and in the knowledge of our Lord and Saviour Jesus Christ. To him be glory both now and for ever. Amen." 2 Peter 3:18

Pious talk doesn't mean a thing unless it is coming from a pious heart.
— Touching Heaven, 1991

"Charity suffereth long, and is kind; charity envieth not; charity vaunteth not itself, is not puffed up," 1 Corinthians 13:4

SORROW

The whole world is in sorrow.
— "The Hallelujah Chorus" In One Verse, 1996

"The impotent man answered him, Sir, I have no man, when the water is troubled, to put me into the pool: but while I am coming, another steppeth down before me." John 5:7

SOULWINNING

It takes courage to be a soulwinner.
— "The Hallelujah Chorus" In One Verse, 1996

"Wait on the LORD: be of good courage, and he shall strengthen thine heart: wait, I say, on the LORD." Psalms 27:14

Give the gospel, my friend, for by your giving, your salvation becomes bigger and better. The more you share, the more you will enjoy that which God has done for you.
— The Witness Book, 1965

"He that goeth forth and weepeth, bearing precious seed, shall doubtless come again with rejoicing, bringing his sheaves with him." Psalms 126:6

A "live" church has an aggressive, evangelistic spirit. Evangelism is the key spirit.
— A Winner Never Quits and A Quitter Never Wins, 1994
"And daily in the temple, and in every house, they ceased not to teach and preach Jesus Christ." Acts 5:42

We cannot discuss the great commission without remembering that God's divine purpose is to bring people unto Himself.
— Start the Fire, 1986
"Go ye into all the world, and preach the gospel to every creature." Mark 16:15

Suffering, persecution, and death scattered the blaze of gospel fire.
— Are You Tired of Living?, 1945
"...bonds and afflictions abide me. But none of these things move me, neither count I my life dear unto myself, so that I might finish my course with joy, and the ministry, which I have received of the Lord Jesus, to testify the gospel of the grace of God." Acts 20:23-24

We who are workers for Christ must remember that we cannot always reap, but we must sow as well.
— Some Golden Daybreak, 1996
"Behold, the husbandman waiteth for the precious fruit of the earth, and hath long patience for it, until he receive the early and latter rain. Be ye also patient; stablish your hearts: for the coming of the Lord draweth nigh." James 5:7-8

The average Christian is not going out to win others to Christ until he is sent out by a driving force.
— Are You Tired of Living?, 1945
"For though I preach the gospel, I have nothing to glory of: for necessity is laid upon me; yea, woe is unto me, if I preach not the gospel!" 1 Corinthians 9:16

Two things that are necessary for life: a goal and a guide.

— *Start The Fire, 1986*

"I can do all things through Christ which strengtheneth me." Philippians 4:13

"To this end was I (Christ) born, and for this cause came I into the world, that I should bear witness unto the truth. Every one that is of the truth heareth my voice." John 18:37

We need anointed lips to speak what Jesus commands us to speak. We must know the message, exemplify the message and tell the message.

— *This Crisis Hour, 1991*

"And he said unto them, Go ye into all the world, and preach the gospel to every creature." Mark 16:15

There are no exceptions and no exemptions, God has spoken once and for all upon this subject. He tells us, "Ye shall be witnesses unto me."

— *Start the Fire, 1986*

"But ye shall receive power, after that the Holy Ghost is come upon you: and ye shall be witnesses unto me both in Jerusalem, and in all Judaea, and in Samaria, and unto the uttermost part of the earth." Acts 1:8

Sowing the Word is a heavenly task, for by giving the message of Christ, we are getting people ready for eternity and heaven."

— *Start the Fire, 1986*

Go ye therefore, and teach all nations, baptizing them in the name of the Father, and of the Son, and of the Holy Ghost: Teaching them to observe all things whatsoever I have commanded you: and, lo, I am with you alway, even unto the end of the world. Amen." Matthew 28:19-20

There is nothing more wonderful to behold than the earnestness and enthusiasm of a new Christian, going after lost people.
— Start the Fire, 1986

"He first findeth his own brother Simon, and saith unto him, We have found the Messias, which is, being interpreted, the Christ. And he brought him to Jesus." John 1:41-42

Turning men to Christ requires prayer, alertness, spirit, tears, and faithfulness.
— Start the Fire, 1986

"He that goeth forth and weepeth, bearing precious seed, shall doubtless come again with rejoicing, bringing his sheaves with him." Psalms 126:6

Our Heavenly Father was the first to enter the advertising business. Centuries ago he advertised for a man in this way: "Whom shall I send and who will go for us? Isaiah 6:8
— Start the Fire, 1986

To win men to Christ, we must realize three things:
The lostness of men,
The power of the Savior, and
The willingness of God.
— The Big 90, 1999

"The Lord is not slack concerning his promise, as some men count slackness; but is longsuffering to us-ward, not willing that any should perish, but that all should come to repentance." 2 Peter 3:9

Our love should drive us out in service for Christ. There is an old proverb which says, "He who has love in his heart has spurs in his side." Let love explode in your heart and you will be going out as a witness.
— Are You Tired Of Living?, 1945
"For the love of Christ constraineth us; because we thus judge, that if one died for all, then were all dead:" 2 Corinthians 5:14

SPEECH

A small amount of conversation can affect a great number of people.
— "The Hallelujah Chorus" In One Verse, 1996
"Let the words of my mouth, and the meditation of my heart, be acceptable in thy sight, O LORD, my strength, and my redeemer." Psalms 19:14

STABILITY

Stability is demanded by the Word of God and will be rewarded at the Judgment Seat of Christ.
— Compassion Unlimited
"Therefore, my beloved brethren, be ye stedfast, unmoveable, always abounding in the work of the Lord, forasmuch as ye know that your labour is not in vain in the Lord." 1 Corinthians 15:58

STRENGTH

The world's great have erased the words "I quit" from their vocabularies.
— Are You Tired Of Living, 1945
"I can do all things through Christ which strengtheneth me." Philippians 4:13

SUBMISSION

What a holy hush overtakes any Christian when he considers that word submission!
— Two Dogs and Peace of Mind, 1974

"Saying, Father, if thou be willing, remove this cup from me: nevertheless not my will, but thine, be done." Luke 22:42

Submission brings an understanding of the Word of God, happiness in worship, peace of heart, and gives your life an influence for good.
— The Key To a Changed Life, 1978

"And the peace of God, which passeth all understanding, shall keep your hearts and minds through Christ Jesus." Philippians 4:7

If I wait upon God in submissiveness — which is the key — I can take my hands off and say, "Lord, here I am."
— The Key To Victorious Living, 1978

"Submit yourselves therefore to God. Resist the devil, and he will flee from you." James 4:7

SUCCESS

Christians fail because of stubbornness, ignorance, fleshly weakness, and unwillingness to die to self, and an unwillingness to take of the fullness of the Spirit of God.
— The Key To Victorious Living, 1978

"For ye are dead, and your life is hid with Christ in God." Colossians 3:3

The successful life is wholly indentified with Christ, obedient to the Word of God, busy and working, a blessing to others and a life with a burden.
— The Big 90, 1999
"I beseech you therefore, brethren, by the mercies of God, that ye present your bodies a living sacrifice, holy, acceptable unto God, which is your reasonable service." Romans 12:1

Men may build what they feel is a good life -- spend much time in hard work -- striving, and then find that it is nothing. Too often the attainments bring little joy because of that which happens in the hour of fruition.
— Ten Thousand Tears, 1980
"But seek ye first the kingdom of God, and his righteousness; and all these things shall be added unto you." Matthew 6:33

I can usually tell when a man is going to make a success in doing a certain task. If his body is alert, and his eye has a sparkle and if he is sort of leaning forward, anxious, ready, and enthusiastic, he is going to do something!
— Are You Tired Of Living? 1945
"Not slothful in business; fervent in spirit; serving the Lord;" Romans 12:11

SUCCESSFUL LIVING

Thousands have found the secret of happy, successful living in the midst of life's deepest despair.
— Are You Tired Of Living? 1945
"Be not overcome of evil, but overcome evil with good." Romans 12:21

SUFFERING

Greatness comes from men who have gone through suffering.

— Fireworks Don't Last, 1982

"But the God of all grace, who hath called us unto his eternal glory by Christ Jesus, after that ye have suffered a while, make you perfect, stablish, strengthen, settle you." 1 Peter 5:10

SURRENDER

We cannot follow Christ in all ways — why? The limitations of the flesh. He was the incarnate Son of God. He was perfect, sinless, and holy. We are weak, finite, and carnal.

— Start the Fire, 1986

"For he hath made him to be sin for us, who knew no sin; that we might be made the righteousness of God in him." 2 Corinthians 5:21

An intense Lee Roberson.

Dr. Lee Roberson is certainly one of the most powerful and persuasive voices for the Christian faith in history. I am very grateful his words have been preserved so that future generations may experience his leadership and know his Lord.

- Jack Graham, Pastor, Prestonwood Baptist Church, Plano, Texas

T

TEACHINGS, JESUS'

Jesus taught more about life than any man who ever lived on earth. He teaches us how to treat our enemies, how to live without worry, how to go on despite all misfortune, and the importance of death itself.
— This Crisis Hour, 1991

"For whether we live, we live unto the Lord; and whether we die, we die unto the Lord: whether we live therefore, or die, we are the Lord's." Romans 14:8

TEAMWORK

Teamwork:
Assures power in prayer.
Assures mutual encouragement.
Carries with it the sharing of responsibility.
Adds force to testimony.
Makes possible the accomplishment of a larger task.
— This Crisis Hour, 1991

"Again I say unto you, That if two of you shall agree on earth as touching any thing that they shall ask, it shall be done for them of my Father which is in heaven." Matthew 18:19

TEMPTATION

We need to know the weakness of the flesh, the temptations of the world, and the power of Satan.
— The Big 90, 1999

"Be sober, be vigilant; because your adversary the devil, as a roaring lion, walketh about, seeking whom he may devour: Whom resist stedfast in the faith, knowing that the same afflictions are accomplished in your brethren that are in the world." 1 Peter 5:8-9

TESTIMONY

Christ demands a positive testimony.
— "The Hallelujah Chorus" In One Verse, 1996
"While we look not at the things which are seen, but at the things which are not seen: for the things which are seen are temporal; but the things which are not seen are eternal." 2 Corinthians 4:18

A positive testimony strengthens others while a weak testimony hurts both family and friends.
— The Faith That Moves Mountains, 1984
"But whoso shall offend one of these little ones which believe in me, it were better for him that a millstone were hanged about his neck, and that he were drowned in the depth of the sea." Matthew 18:6

We must not compromise to avoid criticism.
— Preaching to America, 1999
"For even hereunto were ye called: because Christ also suffered for us, leaving us an example, that ye should follow his steps:" 1 Peter 2:21

The positive light shines by purity of life, positive action, and consistency.
— Coming To Chattanooga...Soon, 1980
"Let your light so shine before men, that they may see your good works, and glorify your Father which is in heaven." Matthew 5:16

God is glorified by a positive testimony. Satan gains when a testimony is limp and hesitatingly given.
— Preaching to America, 1999
"And I thank Christ Jesus our Lord, who hath enabled me, for that he counted me faithful, putting me into the ministry;" 1 Timothy 1:12

Our words should testify to His saving grace.
— It's Dynamite, 1953
"Let the redeemed of the LORD say so" Psalms 107:2

TESTING

Our Lord is always testing people, testing in order to help.
He tests us that we might know ourselves.
He tests us to strengthen us.
He tests us to destroy all self-sufficiency.
— The Faith That Moves Mountains, 1984
"For he knoweth our frame; he remembereth that we are dust." Psalms 103:14

May we learn to spread each difficulty before the Lord. May we remember that we are nothing, but He is everything; we are feeble, but He is strong; our resources are limited, but His are limitless.
— The Faith That Moves Mountains, 1984
"I can do all things through Christ which strengtheneth me." Philippians 4:13

THOUGHTS

Remember: you can have just one thought at a time, and it will be either good or bad. So read the right things. Put good things into your mind.
— Preaching To America, 1999
"Finally, brethren, whatsoever things are true, whatsoever things are honest, whatsoever things are just, whatsoever things are pure, whatsoever things are lovely, whatsoever things are of good report; if there be any virtue, and if there be any praise, think on these things." Philippians 4:8

Almost everything in life depends on your thoughts.
— Two Dogs and Peace of Mind, 1974
"For as he thinketh in his heart, so is he." Proverbs 23:7

The Lord has given us prayer to be a guide toward thought control.
— Two Dogs and Peace Of Mind, 1974
"For it is sanctified by the word of God and prayer." 1 Timothy 4:5

TRIALS

Quite often trials follow the victories of life.
— Two Dogs and Peace of Mind, 1974
"Wherefore let him that thinketh he standeth take heed lest he fall."
1 Corinthians 10:12

The trials and the strains of life are inwardly in single file, as that coming from the top to the bottom of an hour glass, depicting the passage of time.
— Fireworks Don't Last, 1982
"So teach us to number our days, that we may apply our hearts unto wisdom."
Psalms 90:12

TROUBLE

Difficulties do three things for us: they test us, train us, and toughen us.
— People: A Book About Bible People, 1983
"As yet I am as strong this day as I was in the day that Moses sent me: as my strength was then, even so is my strength now, for war, both to go out, and to come in."
Joshua 14:11-12

Troubles of life knock off the rough edges and give us a better understanding of God's will, a submissiveness of spirit to do what God want us to do.
— The Big 90, 1999

"Yea, though I walk through the valley of the shadow of death, I will fear no evil: for thou art with me; thy rod and thy staff they comfort me. Thou preparest a table before me in the presence of mine enemies: thou anointest my head with oil; my cup runneth over." Psalms 23:4-5

The gravest trouble is always the present trouble, and your present trouble will remain until a new one arrives.
— The Faith That Moves Mountains, 1984

"God is our refuge and strength, a very present help in trouble." Psalms 46:1

What makes people great? Trouble borne in the Spirit of Christ.
— The Big 90, 1999

"And he said unto me, My grace is sufficient for thee:" 2 Corinthians 12:9

The most beautiful songs come out of the heartaches of life.
— The Big 90, 1999

"But none saith, Where is God my maker, who giveth songs in the night;" Job 35:10

Trouble magnifies our weakness and God's power.
— People: A Book About Bible People, 1983

"And he said unto me, My grace is sufficient for thee: for my strength is made perfect in weakness. Most gladly therefore will I rather glory in my infirmities, that the power of Christ may rest upon me. Therefore I take pleasure in infirmities, in reproaches, in necessities, in persecutions, in distresses for Christ's sake: for when I am weak, then am I strong." 2 Corinthians 12:9-10

Dr. Roberson visits the campus of Crown College in Powell, Tennessee.

Lee Roberson can say more in a sentence than most of us can say in a page. Every sentence is a brilliant diamond, sparkling with profound truth. Don't miss having this treasure.

- Bailey Smith, Author, Evangelist, past President, Southern Baptist Convention

U

UNBELIEF

Unbelief is the sin that condemns me.
— This Crisis Hour, 1991

"He that believeth on him is not condemned: but he that believeth not is condemned already, because he hath not believed in the name of the only begotten Son of God." John 3:18

Unbelief damns the souls of men: therefore, shun unbelief as you would an awful, contagious disease.

"And Jesus answering saith unto them, Have faith in God." Mark 11:22

UNCERTAINTY

Uncertainty is a part of this present time, but the uncertainty of life causes us to build our lives on the solid rock Christ Jesus.
— Compassion Unlimited,

"Whereas ye know not what shall be on the morrow. For what is your life? It is even a vapour, that appeareth for a little time, and then vanisheth away. For that ye ought to say, If the Lord will, we shall live, and do this, or that." James 4:14-15

Dr. and Mrs. Roberson on the campus of Crown College in Powell, TN.

Dr. Lee Roberson is one of my heroes in the faith. God has given him a remarkable ministry. Thanks to Lindsay Terry for providing this presentation of the wit and wisdom of Lee Roberson.

- Jerry Vines, former Pastor, First Baptist Church, Jacksonville, Florida, and past President, Southern Baptist Convention

V

VICTORIOUS LIVING

The defeated life is dominated by the world, the flesh and the Devil — three enemies who work for the constant defeat of a Christian.
— The Faith That Moves Mountains, 1984
"Wherefore come out from among them, and be ye separate, saith the Lord, and touch not the unclean thing; and I will receive you," 2 Corinthians 6:17

We must live victoriously to be obedient to His commandments. Defeated Christians disgrace the cause of Christ.
— "The Hallelujah Chorus" In One Verse, 1996
"But thanks be to God, which giveth us the victory through our Lord Jesus Christ." 1 Corinthians 15:57

The besetting sin will defeat you in your quest for peace. Your conscience and the Holy Spirit will hold it up before you.
— Are You Tired Of Living? 1945
"...let us lay aside every weight, and the sin which doth so easily beset us, and let us run with patience the race that is set before us," Hebrews 12:1

VICTORY

The world loves a winner. A good loser may be popular for a time, but eventually his place will be taken by a winner. We like to see a man win in the battle of life. He may not attain to riches or popular glory, but there is something about him that proclaims he is a winner.
— A Winner Never Quits and A Quitter Never Wins, 1994
"I have fought a good fight, I have finished my course, I have kept the faith:" 2 Timothy 4:7

A man can know when he has won in the battle of life. This is not egotism. This is the sense of understanding what God wanted him to do and a knowledge that the task has been done. Paul had an inner feeling of peace that always comes to the one who does his best.

— *A Winner Never Quits and A Quitter Never Wins,* 1994

"It is God that girdeth me with strength, and maketh my way perfect." Psalm 18:32

VIGILANCE

Satan will walk, not only into any church or any home, but into any life.

— *Start the Fire,* 1986

"Put on the whole armour of God, that ye may be able to stand against the wiles of the devil." Ephesians 6:11

VISION

We need anointed eyes to see what Jesus saw.

— *The Crisis Hour,* 1991

"Say not ye, There are yet four months, and then cometh harvest? behold, I say unto you, Lift up your eyes, and look on the fields; for they are white already to harvest." John 4:35

Dr. Lee Roberson has been one of my mentors for many years. I have always found him ready and willing to help in any way possible. As a pastor I have sent many students from our church to Tennessee Temple University, assured in my own mind that they would get a wonderful education in a Christian atmosphere, and that they would be greatly benefited as they sat under the influence of this giant of the faith.

Dr. Roberson has been faithful and true to the vision God has given him. He is truly an excellent role model for Christians who want to serve the Lord.

- Gary Coleman, past Moderator, Southwide Baptist Fellowship, Pastor, Lavon Drive Baptist Church, Garland, Texas

WISDOM

It may sound pious but not intelligent to say that you never read any book but the Bible. To the contrary, the Bible encourages us to be "as wise as serpents and as harmless as doves."
— Are You Tired of Living? 1945

"Behold, I send you forth as sheep in the midst of wolves: be ye therefore wise as serpents, and harmless as doves." Matthew 10:16

Wise people make ready for two certain events — death and the second coming of Christ.
— A Winner Never Quits and A Quitter Never Wins, 1994

"Watch therefore, for ye know neither the day nor the hour wherein the Son of man cometh." Matthew 25:13

The lost sometimes have more perception of certain matters than Christians.
— A Winner Never Quits and A Quitter Never Wins, 1994

"...the children of this world are in their generation wiser than the children of light." Luke 16:8

WITNESS

A man who has a genuine case of salvation is going to want to talk about it.
— Are You Tired Of Living?, 1945

"But his word was in mine heart as a burning fire shut up in my bones, and I was weary with forbearing, and I could not stay." Jeremiah 20:9

WORK

God's method is men! When He has a job to do, He selects one for that task.

— This Crisis Hour, 1991

"And I sought for a man among them, that should make up the hedge, and stand in the gap before me for the land, that I should not destroy it: but I found none." Ezekiel 22:30

WORLD (THE)

We must make distinctions in how we use the word "world." We have the world of nature, the world of man, and the world of sin and rebellion.

— "The Hallelujah Chorus" In One Verse, 1996

"For Demas hath forsaken me, having loved this present world" 2 Timothy 4:10

The world is against God.

— "The Hallelujah Chorus" In One Verse, 1996

"And we know that we are of God, and the whole world lieth in wickedness." 1 John 5:19

The world is dangerous, deceptive and deadly. It is Satan-controlled and is against all that is godly. It is explosive dynamite.

— "The Hallelujah Chorus" In One Verse, 1996

"Lest Satan should get an advantage of us: for we are not ignorant of his devices." 2 Corinthians 2:11

WORLDLINESS

Christians are kept from victory and real service because of selfishness and greed of worldly things.

— Are You Tired Of Living? 1945

"He also that received seed among the thorns is he that heareth the word; and the care of this world, and the deceitfulness of riches, choke the word, and he becometh unfruitful." Matthew 13:22

WORRY

Sinful man is by nature a worrier. It is only when man takes hold of the promises of God by faith that worry slips away. Surely God delights in that man or woman who by simple faith achieves perfect peace and rest of heart.

— It's Dynamite, 1953

"Casting all your care upon him; for he careth for you." 1 Peter 5:7

Worry is sin.

— It's Dynamite, 1953

"Be careful for nothing; but in every thing by prayer and supplication with thanksgiving let your requests be made known unto God." Philippians 4:6

Eliminate those things which are useless to worry about.

— The Faith That Moves Mountains, 1984

"In the multitude of thy thoughts within me thy comforts delight my soul." Psalm 94:19

There are first-class and second-class troubles. If you are going to have worries, let them be large, decent, respectable, aristocratic worries.

"And he said unto me, My grace is sufficient for thee: for my strength is made perfect in weakness. Most gladly therefore will I rather glory in my infirmities, that the power of Christ may rest upon me." 2 Corinthians 12:9

WORSHIP

When we worship God, we see Him, and we see His purpose for our lives.

—— 7 Life Changing Statements, 1972

"For we...worship God in the spirit, and rejoice in Christ Jesus, and have no confidence in the flesh." Philippians 3:3

True worship gives direction for your life.

—— 7 Life Changing Statements, 1972

"And he hath put a new song in my mouth, even praise unto our God: many shall see it, and fear, and shall trust in the LORD." Psalms 40:3

True worship gives strength in times of weakness.

—— 7 Life Changing Statements, 1972

"For the LORD God is a sun and shield: the LORD will give grace and glory: no good thing will he withhold from them that walk uprightly." Psalms 84:11

True worship gives an overwhelming consciousness of the greatness of our salvation.

—— 7 Life Changing Statements, 1972

"Thanks be unto God for his unspeakable gift." 2 Corinthians 9:15

Worshiping God is holy, blessed, good, and wise. God has so ordained by the Bible that we worship Him.
— Fireworks Don't Last, 1982

"Give unto the LORD the glory due unto his name; worship the LORD in the beauty of holiness." Psalms 29:2

As we come to worship our God, we must always be calling upon Him for the cleansing of our hearts.
— 7 Life Changing Statements, 1972

"Having therefore these promises, dearly beloved, let us cleanse ourselves from all filthiness of the flesh and spirit, perfecting holiness in the fear of God." 2 Corinthians 7:1

Worship gives us courage, makes prayer a power, makes God's promises a reality, and changes our attitudes.
— 7 Life Changing Statements, 1972

"For the LORD God is a sun and shield: the LORD will give grace and glory: no good thing will he withhold from them that walk uprightly." Psalms 84:11

Preaching to the people of HPBC.

When I think of a life well-lived, the name Dr. Lee Roberson comes to mind. What an influence he has been in my life and thousands and thousands of others. I believe that those who read his works will be touched like all the rest of us.

- Johnny Hunt, Pastor, First Baptist Church, Woodstock, Georgia

Y

YOUTH

Youth must be directed; and if youth be misspent, then all of life is wasted.
— The Gold Mine, 1996

"Let no man despise thy youth; but be thou an example of the believers, in word, in conversation, in charity, in spirit, in faith, in purity." 1 Timothy 4:12

Day after day in the chapel services, and weekly in sermons at Highland Park Baptist Church, he stood for Christ Jesus: stood with clarity and confidence, in a way that manifestly claimed the world for Christ. It was more than religion. It was life. He was not just a CEO or a president or a pastor, but one who established a context of Christ's living water that brought the presence of God to all around him. Dr. Roberson, "I thank my God on every remembrance of you."

- Dallas Willard, Author, Professor, University of Southern California School of Philosophy

Dr. Roberson greeting the international students in the early days of Tennesee Temple.

BOOKS BY LEE ROBERSON

Some of the books below are out of print but can be purchased from www.abebooks.com or www.barnesandnoble.com in the out-of-print section.

Dr. Roberson had numerous articles published in leading periodicals in America. Multiplied thousands of cassette tapes of his sermons have been distributed.

A Winner Never Quits and
A Quitter Never Wins
Sword of the Lord Publishers, 1994

Are You Tired of Living?
University Publishers, 1945, renewed in 1986

Behold He Comes
University Publishers, 1990

Camp Joy Scrap Book
Lee Roberson, 1977

Coming to Chattanooga -- Soon
Sword of the Lord Publishers, 1980

Compassion Unlimited
Johnson Printing Company

Death and After
Lee Roberson, 1954

Diamonds In the Rough
Sword of the Lord Publishers, 1997

Disturbing Questions...
Solid Answers
Sword of the Lord Publishers, 1978

Double-Breasted
Sword of the Lord Publishers, 2000

Endued With Power
Hebrew Christian Fellowship

Fireworks Don't Last
University Publishers, 1982

Five Ancient Sins
Sword of the Lord Publishers, 1954

For Preachers Only
Sword of the Lord Publishers, 1973

How to Get the Biggest
Bargain In Town
Lee Roberson, 1968

It's Dynamite
Sword of the Lord Publishers, 1953

Kings On Parade
Sword of the Lord Publishers, 1956

Mr. Saint and Mr. Sinner
Golden Rule Press, 1963

One Man's Convictions
Lee Roberson, 1972

Pastor's Fourth Anniversary
Highland Park Baptist Church, 1946

PEOPLE: A Book About
Bible People
Bible & Literature Missionary Foundation, 1983

Prayer: Life Changing Sermons
Lee Roberson, 1956

Preaching to America
Sword of the Lord Publishers, 1999

Scrap Book In A Day
Compiled by Lee Roberson

7 Life Changing Statements
Lee Roberson, 1972

Some Golden Daybreak
Sword of the Lord Publishers, 1957

Start the Fire
University Publishers, 1986

Ten Thousand Tears
Sword of the Lord Publishers, 1980

The Big 90
Sword of the Lord Publishers, 1999

The Faith That Moves Mountains
Sword of the Lord Publishers, 1984

The Gold Mine
Sword of the Lord Publishers, 1996

The Golden Link
Zondervan Bible Publishers, 1959

"The Hallelujah Chorus"
In One Verse
John the Baptist Publishers, 1996

The Key to A Changed Life
Sword of the Lord Publishers, 1978

The Key to Victorious Living
University Publications, 1978

The King's Water Boy
Lee Roberson

The Man in Cell No. 1
Sword of the Lord Publishers, 2000

The University of Hard Knocks
The Golden Rule Press, 1960

The Witness Book
Christ for the World Publishers, 1965

The World's Best Holiday
Sword of the Lord Publishers, 1974

This Crisis Hour
University Publishers, 1991

Three In One: Be Filled With
The Spirit, The Golden Link, and
Peace and Joy In the Believer's Life
Highland Park Baptist Church

Touching Heaven
Sword of the Lord Publishers, 1991

Two Dogs and Peace of Mind
Sword of the Lord Publishers, 1974

AFTERWORD

Lee Roberson Foundation

The purpose of the Lee Roberson Foundation is to provide post secondary tuition scholarships to Christian men and women who have exemplified outstanding qualities of character, leadership and scholarship.

The Foundation has been established by the children of Dr. Lee Roberson as a continuing legacy of their father's love for Christian men and women who aspire to attain the highest level of educational preparedness available to them. While they recognize all the accomplishments of their father with great admiration, it is their father's untiring efforts to raise money for the scholarship programs during his years of leadership at Tennessee Temple University that has inspired the establishment of the Lee Roberson Foundation.

Disbursements of the awarded scholarships are administered through the Financial Aids departments of designated colleges and universities. Donors to the Foundation are welcome to designate the institution(s) of their choice where they want the Lee Roberson Foundation scholarship(s) to be available.

The directors of the Lee Roberson Foundation are delighted to commission a limited edition publication of this anthology of Dr. Roberson's wisdom and wit. Lindsay Terry is commended for his vision for this book and his efforts to make it a reality.

For more information about the Lee Roberson Foundation, applications for scholarships, how to make a tax deductible donation to the Foundation and other works by Dr. Lee Roberson, call 1-800-778-7887 or go to www.leeroberson.org.